Diseases and Disorders

Hepatitis

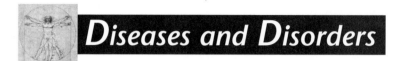
Diseases and Disorders

Hepatitis

Titles in the Diseases and Disorders series include:

Diseases and Disorders

Hepatitis

by Barbara Sheen

LUCENT
BOOKS®

THOMSON
™
GALE

San Diego • Detroit • New York • San Francisco • Cleveland
New Haven, Conn. • Waterville, Maine • London • Munich

THOMSON
™
GALE

© 2003 by Lucent Books. Lucent Books is an imprint of The Gale Group, Inc.,
a division of Thomson Learning, Inc.

Lucent Books® and Thomson Learning™ are trademarks used herein under license.

For more information, contact
Lucent Books
27500 Drake Rd.
Farmington Hills, MI 48331-3535
Or you can visit our Internet site at http://www.gale.com

LIBRARY OF CONGRESS CATALOGING-IN-PUBLICATION DATA

Sheen Barbara.
    Hepatitis / by Barbara Sheen.
v. cm. — (Diseases and disorders)
Includes bibliographical references and index.
Contents: Introduction: A silent threat to individuals and society — What is hepatitis?
— Diagnosis and treatment — Alternative treatments — Living with hepatitis — What
the future holds.
    ISBN 1-59018-041-0 (hardback : alk. paper)
    1. Hepatitis—Juvenile literature. [1. Hepatitis. 2. Diseases.] I. Title. II. Diseases and dis-
orders series.
    RC848.H42 S447 2003
    616.3'623—dc21

                                                                    2002003587

Printed in the United States of America

Table of Contents

"The Most Difficult Puzzles Ever Devised"

CHARLES BEST, ONE of the pioneers in the search for a cure for diabetes, once explained what it is about medical research that intrigued him so. "It's not just the gratification of knowing one is helping people," he confided, "although that probably is a more heroic and selfless motivation. Those feelings may enter in, but truly, what I find best is the feeling of going toe to toe with nature, of trying to solve the most difficult puzzles ever devised. The answers are there somewhere, those keys that will solve the puzzle and make the patient well. But how will those keys be found?"

Since the dawn of civilization, nothing has so puzzled people—and often frightened them, as well—as the onset of illness in a body or mind that had seemed healthy before. A seizure, the inability of a heart to pump, the sudden deterioration of muscle tone in a small child—being unable to reverse such conditions or even to understand why they occur was unspeakably frustrating to healers. Even before there were names for such conditions, even before they were understood at all, each was a reminder of how complex the human body was, and how vulnerable.

While our grappling with understanding diseases has been frustrating at times, it has also provided some of humankind's most heroic accomplishments. Alexander Fleming's accidental discovery in 1928 of a mold that could be turned into penicillin has resulted in the saving of untold millions of lives. The isolation of the enzyme insulin has reversed what was once a death sentence for anyone with diabetes. There have been great strides in combating conditions for which there is not yet a cure, too. Medicines can help AIDS patients live longer, diagnostic tools such as mammography and ultrasounds can help doctors find tumors while they are treatable, and laser surgery techniques have made the most intricate, minute operations routine.

This "toe-to-toe" competition with diseases and disorders is even more remarkable when seen in a historical continuum. An astonishing amount of progress has been made in a very short time. Just two hundred years ago, the existence of germs as a cause of some diseases was unknown. In fact, it was less than 150 years ago that a British surgeon named Joseph Lister had difficulty persuading his fellow doctors that washing their hands before delivering a baby might increase the chances of a healthy delivery (especially if they had just attended to a diseased patient)!

Each book in Lucent's *Diseases and Disorders* series explores a disease or disorder and the knowledge that has been accumulated (or discarded) by doctors through the years. Each book also examines the tools used for pinpointing a diagnosis, as well as the various means that are used to treat or cure a disease. Finally, new ideas are presented—techniques or medicines that may be on the horizon.

Frustration and disappointment are still part of medicine, for not every disease or condition can be cured or prevented. But the limitations of knowledge are being pushed outward constantly; the "most difficult puzzles ever devised" are finding challengers every day.

A Silent Threat to Individuals and Society

Eric was a seventeen-year-old high school student when he received a letter from the Red Cross telling him that he could not donate blood during his school's annual blood drive because his blood was infected with hepatitis. Like many people, Eric and his parents were unaware of how serious hepatitis could be. His mother recalls, "We weren't sure exactly what it meant, since we didn't know much about hepatitis. But we set about educating ourselves."[1]

Eric soon learned that hepatitis is an infection of the liver that, in its mildest form, causes only temporary illness but, in its most aggressive form, can slowly destroy the liver and lead to death. A contagious disease, hepatitis is difficult and costly to treat and has no definite cure.

Often called a silent killer, hepatitis can hide inside an infected person's liver for as many as thirty years without being detected or causing any symptoms, while inflicting significant liver damage. It is estimated that about two-thirds of those infected with hepatitis do not know they have it. As a result many of these people unknowingly pass the disease on to others.

Once someone is exposed to hepatitis the odds are that they will contract it. According to the World Health Organization, hepatitis is one hundred times more infectious than the AIDS virus and affects four times as many Americans as AIDS does. One out of every fifteen people worldwide has hepatitis, making hepatitis the most common blood-borne contagious disease in the world. Yet most people are unaware of how it is spread and the danger it presents. In fact, about 60 percent of all the people with hepatitis are unsure of how they contracted the disease. This lack of knowledge about hepatitis and its seriousness, combined with

The hepatitis virus, seen through an electron microscope, causes disease in one out of every fifteen people worldwide.

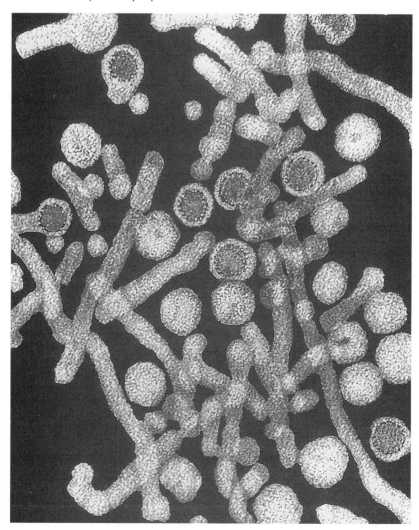

the large number of people who have it, make hepatitis a grave health risk to everyone.

Because hepatitis is one of the most widespread diseases in the world, it not only causes problems for individuals with the disease but also has a huge impact on society. In some parts of the world, such as Southeast Asia, more than half the population will become infected with hepatitis sometime within their lives. Forty million people in India alone currently suffer from hepatitis. The statistics are just as grim in Africa where 72 percent of the people in Tanzania, for example, are infected with hepatitis. But hepatitis is not restricted to people on these continents alone. Over 550 million people worldwide are afflicted with hepatitis. It affects people of every age, gender, and racial group on every continent. Of these, over a half million Americans are infected yearly. Experts estimate that hepatitis's cost to society in medical expenses and work lost is over $600 million per year. This sum does not include the millions spent for liver transplants, of which hepatitis is the leading cause.

Making matters worse, the problem is growing. Some health officials have labeled hepatitis a ticking time bomb. According to the Centers for Disease Control, the number of people infected with hepatitis and the mortality rate caused by the disease is projected to triple in the next fifteen years. Because people are living longer, and hepatitis can hide undetected in people's livers for a number of years, many infected people will find out about their infection in the next two decades as significant liver problems start to occur. By 2010 hepatitis is expected to cause three times as many deaths as AIDS in the United States.

Compounding matters is the expanding prison population in which as many as 40 percent of all inmates are infected. As this population increases, experts predict, so will the spread of the disease among both inmates and prison guards. This contagion will not be contained to the prison community alone, since infected prisoners who return to society are likely to pass the disease on to others.

Despite these statistics, hepatitis receives little attention. As a result, most people do not know very much about it. They are

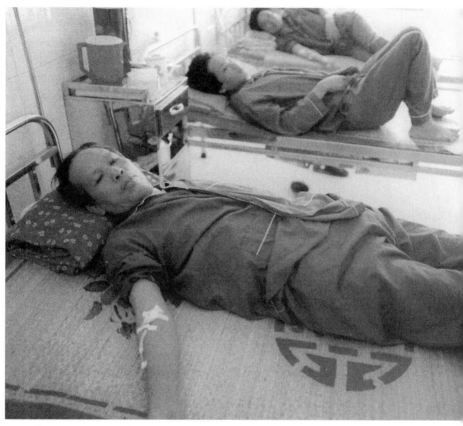

A patient in a Hanoi hospital is treated for hepatitis. In Southeast Asia, more than half the population will become infected with hepatitis sometime in their lives.

unaware of how serious hepatitis can be, what causes it, how the disease is spread, and what steps should be taken to keep from spreading the disease to others. By learning more about hepatitis, and about the behaviors and lifestyle choices that increase the risk of developing it, people can help protect themselves and their loved ones from infection while lessening the damaging effects on society. At the same time, knowing more about hepatitis helps people afflicted with hepatitis to cope better. Also, it helps their friends and family to deal with their fears and misconceptions about how the disease is spread, thus allowing them to provide the support their loved ones need.

Learning about hepatitis allowed Eric to talk about it with his friends, gaining their support while easing their worries of becoming infected too. Currently receiving treatment, Eric is optimistic about the future. "Having hepatitis has changed my life, but not my perspective on life," he explains. "I plan to go to college, to continue my life. Whether or not I have hepatitis, I try to make every day count."[2]

Chapter 1

What Is Hepatitis?

Hepatitis is a disease that inflames and injures the liver, causing it to become swollen and tender. The possible consequence of hepatitis is permanent liver damage. There are seven different varieties of hepatitis. While some varieties are mild and curable, affecting people with no more than a bad case of the flu, other varieties are severe and incurable, resulting in long-term health problems and even death. Despite their differences all seven types of hepatitis are caused by viruses that attack the liver.

Characteristics of the Virus

Viruses are microscopic parasites that invade the body and cause disease and destruction. So small that millions of viruses can fit on the head of a pin, a virus is, according to Nobel laureate Sir Peter Medawar, "A piece of bad news wrapped in protein."[3]

Viruses may enter the body in a number of ways including inhalation, physical contact, through bodily fluids, or in food or water. Once inside the body, the virus's only goal is to reproduce. In order to do this, the virus attaches itself to a healthy host cell that it uses as a home base. The virus's presence prevents the host cell from performing its normal functions and eventually destroys it. The destruction of the host cell, however, does not stop the virus. In a matter of hours, thousands of new viruses are created. The newly formed viruses leave the destroyed host cell and invade other cells where they multiply. Unless the virus is destroyed, this process is repeated over and over again.

Although viruses can invade any cell in the body, different viruses are better equipped to invade different cells. The virus that causes hepatitis always invades liver cells. Scientists are unsure why the hepatitis virus does not invade other organs, but they are sure about the damage it causes. Once the hepatitis virus enters the liver it not only multiplies but often mutates, or changes slightly, causing the newly created viruses to be a little different from the parent virus. This makes it more difficult for the body to fight the hepatitis virus. The immune system must battle not

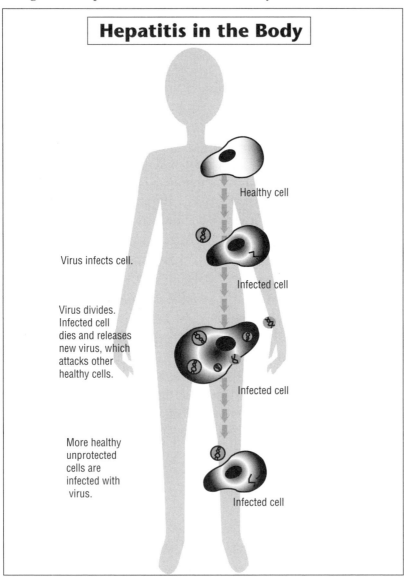

Hepatitis in the Body

Healthy cell

Virus infects cell.

Infected cell

Virus divides. Infected cell dies and releases new virus, which attacks other healthy cells.

Infected cell

More healthy unprotected cells are infected with virus.

Infected cell

one type of hepatitis virus, but many. As a result, in severe cases when the hepatitis virus reproduces and mutates most rapidly, the consequence is often liver failure and death.

What Type of Disease Is Hepatitis?

Hepatitis is an infectious disease that can be spread from person to person. Although some infectious diseases, like the common cold, are spread by casual contact such as sneezing, coughing, or hugging, this is not the case in hepatitis. Depending on its type, hepatitis is spread in three ways: through contact with infected blood, through unprotected sex, and by eating or drinking contaminated food or water.

Complicating matters, though a person may be infected with hepatitis, the virus can hide inside the body for decades causing damage to the liver without producing any symptoms. As a result, these people, known as asymptomatic (meaning they do not show symptoms) carriers, do not know that they are infected with the virus and often unwittingly pass the disease on to others. The effect can be quite dangerous. According to former surgeon general of the United States, C. Everett Koop, "Hepatitis is a disease millions will carry for a decade or more—possibly spreading it to others—while it develops into a serious threat to their health."[4]

Acute or Chronic

In addition to being infectious, hepatitis can be acute or chronic depending on its type. Acute diseases such as the flu have a clear beginning and end, while chronic diseases are long-term with no clear end. Acute hepatitis usually affects patients for about a month and then disappears. A patient who had acute hepatitis explains: "My daughter brought it home from preschool. We all got it. I was the sickest. I had it for over a month. But there was no harm done, I'm completely recovered."[5]

On other hand, the symptoms of chronic hepatitis may come and go, but the hepatitis virus usually is present in patients for the rest of their lives. "It seems like I've had hepatitis forever," a patient with chronic hepatitis explains. "I was diagnosed with it about ten years ago, but I probably walked around with it for a long time before that. Unless they come up with a cure, I'll have it for the rest of my life."[6]

Different Types of Hepatitis

The different types of hepatitis are known as hepatitis A, B, C, D, E, G, and GB. Of these, hepatitis B and C are the most common. About 450 million people throughout the world are afflicted with

Hepatitis A, visible under an electron microscope, is less common than hepatitis B or C.

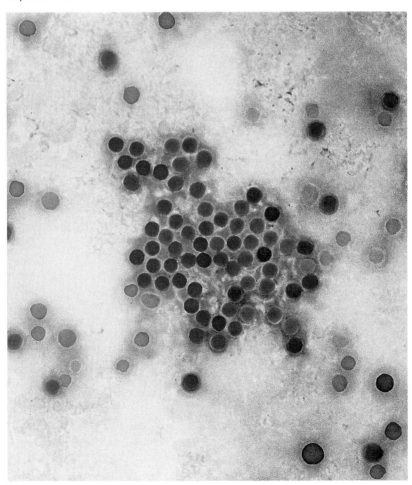

these two diseases. Of these, 4 million Americans suffer from hepatitis C, which was discovered in 1987, and 1.25 million Americans suffer from hepatitis B, which was discovered in 1968. Similar in many ways, both hepatitis B and C can be chronic and incurable.

The main difference between hepatitis B and C is their seriousness. About 80 percent of people exposed to hepatitis C develop chronic hepatitis, while only about 10 percent of those exposed to hepatitis B develop the chronic form of the disease. Experts think this is because the hepatitis C virus multiplies and mutates more rapidly than the hepatitis B virus, making it more dangerous. Consequently, approximately ten thousand people in the United States die from liver failure caused by hepatitis C each year. This is almost double the amount of deaths caused by hepatitis B.

Both hepatitis B and C are transmitted through blood. This can occur when intravenous drug users share contaminated needles, through blood transfusions with contaminated blood, through unprotected sex with an infected partner, and through infected mothers passing the virus on to their babies. A patient with hepatitis C talks about how she thinks she contracted the disease:

> Where did I get Hep C? I was an art student in college, a hippie of sorts, who tried everything that came down the pike, at least once and some much more. I worked for surgeons in the 1970's and I never wore gloves when I cleaned up after office procedures and cleaned instruments. I have five piercings. I had blood during an operation on my hand in the 1980's. I received health department shots with three hundred kids in a line and one shot gun. My ex-husband had Hep C.[7]

Unlike hepatitis B and C, the third most common form of hepatitis, hepatitis A, is always acute, curable, and rarely fatal. Affecting about 125,000 people in the United States each year, hepatitis A is not transmitted through the blood. Instead, this virus is passed through eating or drinking contaminated food or water. For example, eating fruits and vegetables washed in

Ways Hepatitis Is Transmitted

Hepatitis A: oral contact with feces
contaminated food and water

Hepatitis B: contact with infected blood
contaminated needles
infected mother to newborn
sexual contact

Hepatitis C: contact with infected blood
contaminated needles
infected mother to newborn

contaminated water, or shellfish caught in contaminated water, can cause the disease. Food handled by an infected cook or waiter can also spread the disease. This is why signs warning employees to wash their hands are posted in restaurant bathrooms. Oral contact with the feces of infected people can also spread hepatitis A. This most commonly happens in public swimming pools and in nursery schools and daycare centers where young children come in contact with their playmates' infected diapers. Discovered in 1975, hepatitis A frequently occurs as widespread outbreaks in developing countries where sanitation and public health care may be inadequate. Consequently, about 1.4 million people worldwide contract hepatitis A each year. A patient who contracted the disease while traveling talks about her experience:

> I stayed in a very dirty, poor, crowded city. People were not aware of proper food handling, and the government didn't provide many public services. Supermarket workers handled food with their bare hands. Human feces were used as fertilizer, and fruits and vegetables were

sold with fertilizer still on them. Peddlers sold raw oysters on the street. The restaurants washed salad greens in contaminated tap water and used that same water for ice cubes in sodas. It was hard to avoid getting hepatitis. Everybody had it.[8]

Hepatitis D, E, and G are less common forms of hepatitis. Hepatitis D often accompanies and closely resembles hepatitis B. It is more commonly found in the Middle East, Africa, and South America than in the United States since immunization against hepatitis B, which also provides protection against hepatitis D, is not widespread in these regions. Similarly, hepatitis E resembles hepatitis A, and is commonly found in parts of the world with substandard sanitation. Hepatitis G not only resembles hepatitis C, but never infects anyone unless he or she is already infected with hepatitis C. All three diseases are transmitted in the same way and have the same effect on sufferers as the more common forms of hepatitis that they resemble.

Hepatitis GB is the least common form of hepatitis and the most recently discovered. Consequently, little is known about it.

Who Is at Risk?

Although there is no way of predicting who will contract hepatitis, there are some groups, such as young adults, who frequently engage in behaviors that commonly transmit the hepatitis virus and thus are at greater risk. These behaviors include intravenous drug use, sharing cocaine straws, unprotected sex with multiple partners, body piercing, and tattooing. The peak ages, for example, of people who get tattoos in the United States is fourteen through twenty-two. Since tattooing often causes bleeding and involves inserting ink through the skin with a needle-gun that may not be adequately sterilized, it is not uncommon for the hepatitis virus to be passed on in this manner. In fact, studies at the University of Texas Southwestern have shown that young people who have a tattoo are nine times more likely to be infected with hepatitis than people who do not have a tattoo. Body piercing, which is also popular with this age group, involves the breaking of the skin, which may cause bleeding and poses comparable risks.

Experts agree that intravenous drug use is probably the most direct way to contract hepatitis. Users who share needles directly pass the virus into each other's bloodstream. Studies at the University of British Columbia have shown that 60 to 90 percent of all intravenous drug users are infected with hepatitis in just a few months and most are between the ages of eighteen and thirty-five. According to infectious disease expert Dr. Mark Tyndall, "Hepatitis seems to be an occupational hazard among people who inject drugs. Amongst those who are actively using, it seems difficult even among the best-intentioned and the best-informed people to avoid hepatitis. There's such a small number of people that are still negative, it's going to be difficult to change much. Most people are already infected."[9]

Health care workers, who frequently get stuck with infected needles, are another high-risk group. Approximately six hundred thousand health care workers have needle-stick accidents each year, and experts estimate that the chance of getting hepatitis from such accidents is three in one hundred even when workers wear protective gloves. The risk to this group is so great that the Joint Commission on Accreditation of Healthcare Organizations recently issued a national alert in an attempt to help keep health care professionals safe from contamination. An infected health care worker, who found out she had hepatitis during a physical exam, describes how common hepatitis is among her peers: "When I started my career as a medical technician, I got a needle stick. Two years ago, they detected hepatitis. Out of five people in our lab, three ended up with hepatitis."[10]

Travelers to developing countries also have a higher risk of contracting hepatitis, as do people who received blood transfusions before 1992 when scientists learned how to screen donated blood for the hepatitis virus. For these people the risk of infection is one out of every two hundred. However, people who received blood transfusions since blood screening began do not share this risk.

Infants born to mothers infected with hepatitis often contract the disease when their blood intermixes with their mother's. The

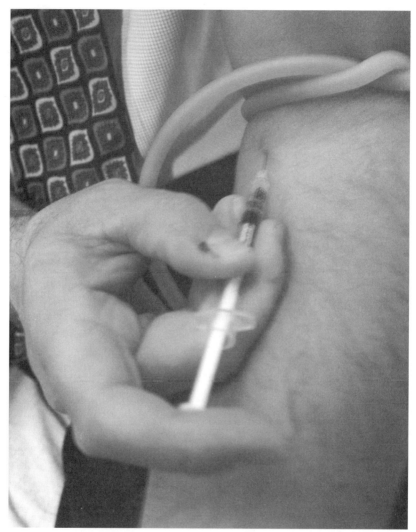

An intravenous drug user is at an extremely high risk of contracting hepatitis.

immune system of these babies does not know that the hepatitis virus does not belong in their bodies and allows the virus to multiply undisturbed. Consequently, these infants have a 90 percent chance of being chronically infected. A mother infected with hepatitis talks about the threat to her daughter: "I tested positive for the hep C, but that was scary enough for me. The scariest part was the possibility that my daughter could have contracted this from me during pregnancy. She was vaccinated for hep B as an infant, but waiting on those test results to see if she tested positive for hep C was a nightmare."[11]

How Many People Are Affected?

No matter how they contract the disease, nearly half of the world's population has had or does have hepatitis. More than 5 million of these sufferers are Americans, and an estimated half million more cases are diagnosed in the United States each year. Although screening of blood for the hepatitis virus before blood transfusions and careful attention to public sanitation is now helping to keep epidemic outbreaks of hepatitis down, this was not always the case. In 1971 and again in 1989 hepatitis A epidemics struck the United States, affecting sixty thousand people. Similar epidemics struck in Mexico City in 1986 and once again in China in 1988, affecting three hundred thousand people. Fortunately, due to a greater understanding of the causes of hepatitis, such epidemic outbreaks seem to be decreasing. However, the overall number of people who have the disease is not. Hepatitis remains the most common blood-borne infection in the United States today. Scientists theorize that this is due to increasing numbers of people engaging in behaviors that can result in infection.

Physical Effects of Hepatitis

Once a person is infected with hepatitis, his or her liver gradually becomes unable to function properly. Since the liver is one of the most important organs in the body, when hepatitis strikes, damage to the liver causes problems throughout the entire body. Located on the right side of the rib cage, the liver is the only organ in the body, other than the skin, that can heal and regenerate itself. With over five hundred jobs, the liver acts like a factory and a warehouse for the body. It turns food into energy by producing a substance known as bile, stores nutrients, and manufactures chemicals that are needed for vital body functions like the clotting of blood. In addition, it purifies the blood, filtering out harmful chemicals made by the body and those found in alcohol, drugs, and pollution. No one can survive without a liver.

The Centers for Disease Control recommends everyone be immunized against hepatitis B. This vaccine, made from a protein that is similar to the hepatitis B virus, creates an immunity to hepatitis B and hepatitis D, which often accompanies hepatitis B. Immunization routinely begins in infants, who are given three injections at four-month intervals. Currently, about 84 percent of all infants in the United States have been vaccinated against hepatitis B. Many states have made proof of immunization a requirement for entering school. In Virginia, for example, all students born in 1994 or later must be vaccinated in order to attend school. County health departments routinely offer children free vaccinations. Protection lasts eleven years. For this reason, young people must be vaccinated again by the age of twelve. Most states have made this a requirement for entering middle school. In Texas, for example, nonimmunized twelve-year-olds are removed from

A California student receives a hepatitis immunization vaccine, which is required by law in some states for school-aged children.

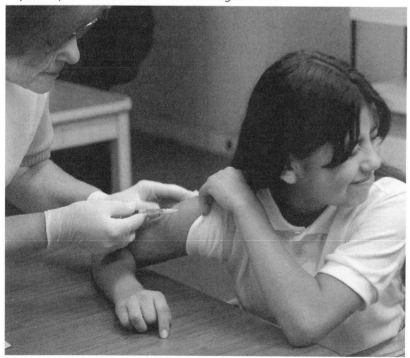

school and prohibited to return until they are vaccinated. Other states, like Virginia, do not allow students to enroll in sixth grade without proof of immunization. These requirements are part of a public health effort to prevent the spread of hepatitis B. According to Jim Farrell, the director of the Division of Immunizations at the Virginia Department of Health, "You never know when someone is going to have a risk factor. At middle school, that is the age when people are entering the high-risk years. Children will be protected by the vaccine as they get older."[12]

Having a healthy lifestyle is another way to prevent contracting hepatitis. Simple hand washing with soap and warm water, for example, is an easy way to help prevent being infected by hepatitis A. Avoiding contact with other people's blood is another way to prevent infection. Sharing personal care products such as razors, toothbrushes, tweezers, fingernail files, and clippers can result in blood-to-blood contact and should be avoided. Users of these products can cut themselves, creating an opening through which infected blood can enter. Experts have found that the hepatitis B and C viruses can live for days on personal grooming items, posing a long-term danger when they are shared. The wife of a hepatitis patient explains how threatening sharing such tools can be: "Yesterday I found my oldest son, a teenager, in front of the bathroom mirror trying to shave for the first time. I got so scared. My husband has hepatitis C. Why didn't we warn him not to borrow his dad's razor?"[13]

Avoiding drug use is another important way to prevent contracting hepatitis. Sharing straws for snorting cocaine or other drugs can cause small blood vessels inside of the nose to break open and bleed, allowing infected blood to be passed on. This can occur even if straws are shared only a few times. Similarly, sharing intravenous drug needles only once can, and often does, result in infection and should be avoided.

Making sure that certified, reputable artists who use sterilized needles do tattoos and body piercing is another way to avoid infection. A hepatitis patient, who contracted the disease as a result of being tattooed with unsterilized needles, explains: "This flag on my arm, I was young and in the Navy. What did I know? Now I'm

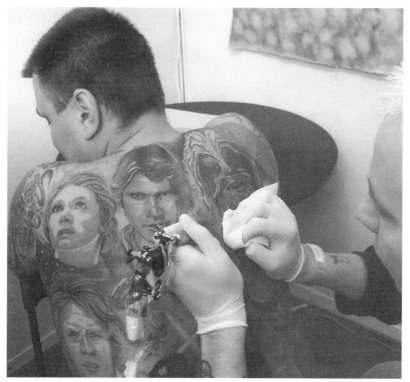

Responsible tattoo artists sterilize their needles after each use to avoid infecting their customers with hepatitis.

told that there are certified tattoo artists, and if you go to someone reputable, everything is sterilized. Well, too late for me."[14]

Finally, avoiding unprotected sex with multiple partners can also prevent infection with hepatitis. This is because the passing of body fluids during unprotected sex can result in the hepatitis virus being spread.

It is clear that although there is no absolute way to prevent being infected by hepatitis, by being immunized and living in a healthy manner people can greatly lessen their chances of contracting this serious infectious disease.

Chapter 2

Diagnosis and Treatment

Hepatitis is a difficult disease to diagnose and treat, making it a challenge to both doctors and patients. The virus can conceal itself inside people for many years without their suspecting they are infected. Even when patients do feel sick, the symptoms can easily be mistaken for other ailments. Complicating matters, tests used to diagnose hepatitis are not always effective and once a diagnosis is made, treatment options are very limited.

Diagnosing Hepatitis

Hepatitis is not always easy to diagnose for many reasons, but largely because many asymptomatic patients do not know they are sick and therefore do not seek help from their doctors. Consequently, they remain undiagnosed for years. Often asymptomatic people are surprised to find out they are infected when their blood is routinely examined during their annual physicals, or when they attempt to donate blood to a blood bank.

According to the American Liver Foundation, in the huge rush to donate blood after the September 11, 2001, terrorist attacks, about 10,000 of 530,000 blood donors discovered that they were infected with hepatitis. Liver specialist Dr. Melissa Palmer talks about Jack, one of her patients, who learned he had hepatitis when he donated blood: "About a week after donating two pints of blood, Jack received a letter from the blood bank stating that they could no longer accept his blood donation—he had tested positive for hepatitis C. Jack could not believe what he was reading. He was in great physical shape! In fact, with the exception of minor colds, he had never really been sick."[15]

Even when patients do have symptoms, the most common symptom is fatigue, which many patients and their doctors attribute to stress, overwork, or depression. According to a patient who had this experience,

> I had hepatitis C, but I didn't know it. My first symptom was fatigue. I was working double shifts, so my doctor thought

A man donates blood at a clinic where his blood will be checked for hepatitis before it is used.

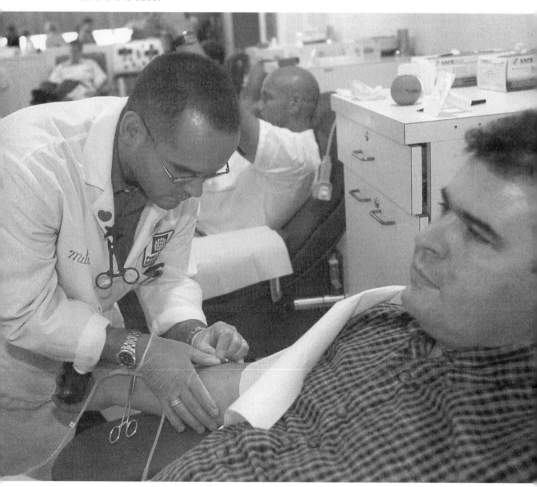

it was overwork, and told me to try to get more rest. Even when things calmed down at work, I was still exhausted. I was spending whatever free time I had horizontal, and it didn't help. When I kept complaining, my doctor pre-scribed an antidepressant. But I wasn't depressed, so it didn't help. When things didn't improve, I went to another doctor for a second opinion. She ran a bunch of blood tests. That's when I found out I had hepatitis.[16]

Other common symptoms so closely resemble those of the flu or mild food poisoning that the possibility of infection with he-patitis is often overlooked. As a result, patients may go for years feeling that something is wrong but not knowing what it is. As one patient explains:

> I had my diagnosis in October 1995. For two years previously I had been feeling unwell—upset stomachs, extreme tiredness, I was losing weight, and I had an almost continuous headache. I decided to get it checked out. They tested me for everything and came up with nothing. A short while later I bumped into a friend who was looking very worried. He told me that he had been diagnosed with hepatitis C and his symptoms were very similar to mine. By this time I was wondering whether I was being a hypochondriac. Anyway, I got it checked out, and the test revealed that I had it.[17]

Symptoms

Although hepatitis symptoms are often difficult to distinguish from other complaints, there are a number of symptoms that point directly to hepatitis. Among these are jaundice, or a yel-lowing of the skin and the whites of the eyes. Jaundice occurs when the liver is unable to eliminate a waste product from the blood called bilirubin, which is made up of old red blood cells. This backup of bilirubin tints the skin and the whites of the eyes yellow; it also turns urine dark brown and feces pale and chalky, two other signs of hepatitis. "I knew something was wrong when I changed my daughter's diaper. The color of the contents was re-

---

Symptoms of Hepatitis

- **Jaundice**
- **Nausea**
- **Dark Urine**
- **Abdominal pain**
- **Light Stools**
- **Loss of appetite**
- **Fatigue**

---

ally weird," a hepatitis patient recalls. "The color of her skin and her eyes were weird too. We took her to the doctor. It was hepatitis A."[18]

Other symptoms that sometimes accompany hepatitis include an itchy skin rash, loss of appetite, and pain around the liver. When these symptoms occur with jaundice they are indicators of liver damage and hepatitis, but when they occur alone they are often mistaken for other problems.

Testing

When symptoms point to hepatitis, several blood tests are usually administered. Specific antibodies, or proteins manufactured by the body to fight bacteria or viruses, commonly are found in the blood of patients with hepatitis A, B, and E. The presence of hepatitis A antibodies, for example, indicates infection with that virus, as does the presence of hepatitis B or E antibodies. The presence of these antibodies is known as the viral load. High viral loads indicate severe infection, while the presence of hepatitis E antibodies suggests that the patient not only is infected but also highly contagious. Experts are unsure why this is so.

Unlike in hepatitis A, B, and E, even when patients are infected with hepatitis C, hepatitis C antibodies may not appear in their blood. This is because the hepatitis C virus is able to hide in the body, infecting victims without being detectable. As a result, the immune system does not form antibodies against the virus. For this reason, when hepatitis C is suspected, other blood tests that measure different liver functions are administered. The most common of these tests is the ALT, or alanine aminotransferase test, which measures levels of alanine aminotransferase, an enzyme or chemical that is produced when the liver is inflamed. The higher the level, the more severe the inflammation. There is also a test that measures bilirubin levels. High levels indicate that the liver is unable to clear bilirubin out of the bloodstream and is not functioning correctly.

Although blood tests are a strong indicator of hepatitis and accompanying liver problems, sometimes a liver biopsy is necessary. It is the only completely reliable method of determining the presence of hepatitis C, and it also provides the most exact diagnosis of the health of the liver. The results of a liver biopsy also help rule out the possibility of other diseases such as liver cancer and provide a reference for evaluating and comparing current

A medical worker draws blood from a patient in order to screen for hepatitis C.

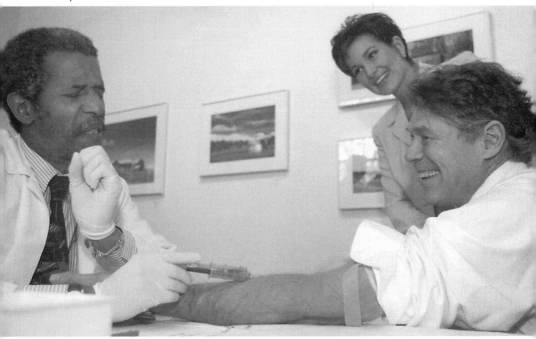

and future liver damage. During a liver biopsy a thin needle is inserted into the liver, and a tiny piece of liver tissue is removed. It's then sent to a laboratory where it is studied under a microscope. To minimize the discomfort caused by the biopsy, patients usually are given a local anesthetic to numb the area. Although the procedure only takes a few minutes, patients must lie still from four to eight hours after the procedure in order to prevent bleeding from the liver. Upon returning home, they are instructed to rest. A patient talks about her experience:

> I had a biopsy done. It wasn't the most pleasant experience in the world, but the team really did their best to make me comfortable. One of the nurses held my hand and talked to me. The most boring part was lying still in the hospital bed with nothing to read or TV to watch for eight hours after the procedure. For the next couple of days I felt like I had been punched in the side, but the painkillers helped and I did return to work the next day. The results of the biopsy showed the virus was active, but not too much permanent damage occurred.[19]

Common Treatments

Once a diagnosis is made, the doctor will evaluate the extent of liver damage and prescribe a treatment accordingly. No matter what form of treatment is prescribed, the goal is to prevent or delay liver damage, maintain current liver functions, and relieve hepatitis symptoms. When the diagnosis indicates that liver damage is minimal, many doctors and patients choose to delay treatment, since hepatitis treatment is often quite unpleasant. If the liver is more severely damaged, treatment with medication usually is prescribed. Unfortunately, there are not many drugs that can effectively treat hepatitis. Few drugs can attack viruses without also damaging the healthy cells that house them. Thus, drugs that are capable of harming the hepatitis virus also significantly harm the liver. Consequently, only a small number of drugs, known as antiviral medications, can be used to treat hepatitis.

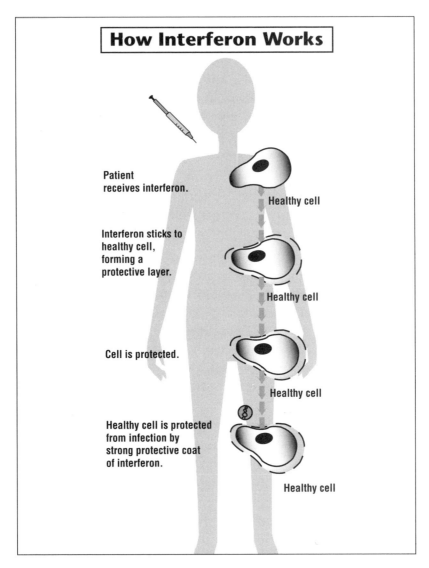

How Interferon Works

Patient receives interferon.

Healthy cell

Interferon sticks to healthy cell, forming a protective layer.

Healthy cell

Cell is protected.

Healthy cell

Healthy cell is protected from infection by strong protective coat of interferon.

Healthy cell

Medication and Its Effects

Currently an antiviral medication known as interferon is the most widely prescribed treatment for hepatitis. Extremely powerful, interferon is a synthetic copy of a protein, also called interferon, which is produced naturally by the body to fight viruses. Interferon works by attaching itself to viruses and blocking them from multiplying without attacking the host cells. Although it is not effective for everyone, interferon may eliminate hepatitis completely in some people, or it may reduce the severity of the virus and slow up liver damage in others.

Administered as an injection, usually by the patients themselves, interferon is injected into the abdomen, thigh, or upper arm three times a week for six months to one year. Many patients are often anxious about this process. One patient recalls:

> I was really nervous about learning how to give myself a shot. When I came into the office, the nurse was looking around for an orange to practice on. She never did find it. So we used a tissue box. It was funny, and it made me laugh—something I never expected to happen.
>
> The first couple of times I did it myself at home, I put the needle in too horizontally. I was going push, push, push and nothing happened. I got awful bruises.
>
> Back to the nurse. She told me to pinch my skin between two fingers, hold the syringe like a dart and go in straight at a 90-degree angle. That worked![20]

Sometimes interferon is combined with another antiviral medication, ribavirin. This treatment consists of three injections of interferon per week and six ribavirin pills a day for six months to two years. Stronger than treatment with interferon alone, this combination treatment is often used on patients whom interferon alone does not help, and on patients who relapse after interferon treatment ends. Although studies have shown that treatment with ribavirin without interferon has no effect on the hepatitis virus, it appears to help interferon fight the virus. According to Dr. Melissa Palmer, "It is not known why ribavirin works against the hepatitis virus only when combined with interferon. However, it has been demonstrated that ribavirin works in union with interferon, boosting interferon's antiviral and immune activity against the hepatitis virus."[21]

Unfortunately neither treatment with interferon alone nor combined treatment helps all patients. After a year of treatment only 20 percent of patients clear the hepatitis virus from their bodies. These patients are known as responders. Thirty percent show a significant decrease in liver damage and hepatitis antibodies, but still remain infected. These patients are known as partial responders. The remaining 50 percent, known as nonresponders, do not respond to treatment at all. Experts believe that antiviral medication is most effective when virus levels in the blood are low.

Health Risks and Side Effects

No matter whether patients respond favorably or unfavorably to interferon treatment, most experience a number of disagreeable side effects that normally accompany the medication. The most common of these are flu-like symptoms such as aches and pains, stiffness, fatigue, fever, chills, headaches, and nausea. Experts believe that these symptoms, which commonly are thought to be produced by the flu virus, actually are produced when the body naturally manufactures interferon to prevent the flu virus from multiplying. Therefore, treatment with synthetic interferon also produces these symptoms. These side effects usually occur four to six hours after an injection and are frequently at their worst early in treatment. A patient explains how his first week of treatment affected him:

> I lay on the couch and started feeling really hot and weak. I got up to go to the bathroom and felt light headed as well. I took my temperature and it was 102F. Then I took an aspirin to reduce the fever but it didn't help. This whole thing lasted about four hours. Then I realized I was feeling better. The next day I felt light headed and feverish, but that was about all. Hey, this was no big deal. The first injection was like having a four-hour average flu. No worse. During the first week, I seemed to be running a fever and my appetite was slightly off. A couple of times I felt kind of nauseous, but not too bad. My energy level was a bit lower. I had a couple of headaches, but they really weren't anything that would stop me from doing things.[22]

Other side effects include hair loss, a metallic taste in the mouth, dry itchy skin, a skin rash, weight loss, depression, and irritability. These occur less frequently but do affect a number of patients. "My hairdresser told me my hair was thinning out," a patient who experienced hair loss recalls. "When I stopped interferon, it all came back."[23]

Surgical Treatment

If the liver becomes so damaged from hepatitis that there's a danger it will cease functioning, neither treatment with interferon nor interferon in combination with ribavirin can help. As a result, a liver transplant may be necessary. Although most hepatitis patients never need a liver transplant, among chronic hepatitis sufferers with cirrhosis, liver failure is possible. When this occurs the only lifesaving treatment is a liver transplant. Currently hepatitis C is the major reason for liver transplants in the United States, accounting for more than one thousand of the four thousand transplants performed each year.

Even when the possibility of liver failure exists, not every patient is considered a good candidate for a liver transplant. Liver transplants are complicated and dangerous, and there is a shortage of donated livers. Moreover, liver transplants are not effective for everyone. Conditions that often result in an unsuccessful liver transplant include advanced heart or lung disease, cancer in an organ other than the liver, being HIV positive, or being a current drug or alcohol abuser. A team of doctors, including a transplant surgeon and a liver specialist, administer a number of tests to possible candidates to ascertain whether a liver transplant is recommended.

Once the team decides a patient is a good candidate for a liver transplant, the patient is put on a waiting list for a liver. Livers for transplant are harvested from patients, known as organ donors, who have agreed to donate their vital organs to others at the time of their death. In many states people who agree to be organ donors sign an organ donor permission statement on their driver's licenses. Unfortunately, there are many more people in need of transplanted livers than there are donors. Although

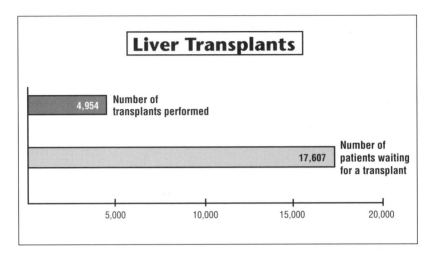

about four thousand liver transplants are performed in the United States each year, about twelve thousand patients are on waiting lists for a liver. More than one quarter of these patients are afflicted with hepatitis.

Because the demand for livers greatly exceeds the supply, once patients are placed on the waiting list the United Network for Organ Sharing ranks them according to how urgent their need is for a transplant. Those with the greatest need are placed on the top of the list. Patients are also classified by their blood type and body size, in order that a compatible liver is found for them. For example, a large man with type B blood needs a liver from a large adult donor with type B blood.

Patients may wait for months or years before a suitable liver is located. As a result, many patients die before a liver is found for them. According to Dr. Paul Grieg, director of liver, kidney, and pancreas transplantation at Toronto General Hospital, "Fifteen to twenty percent of patients die before a liver comes their way. Many of these patients deteriorate substantially on the waiting list. They develop life-threatening complications, are admitted to the hospital and die. As doctors, we say to ourselves the cause of death was waiting."[24]

When a liver is found, transplant surgery can begin. Since a liver transplant is a very complicated operation, many specialists, known as the transplant team, are involved. This team usually includes a hepatologist, or a doctor who specializes in liver disease, a nurse who also specializes in liver disease, a transplant surgeon, and an anesthesiologist who specializes in transplants. The surgery is usually performed in three steps. First, anesthesia is administered so the patient will feel no pain during the operation. Then, the transplant surgeon cuts the patient's abdomen

A surgeon removes a liver during a liver transplant procedure, a last resort for hepatitis sufferers.

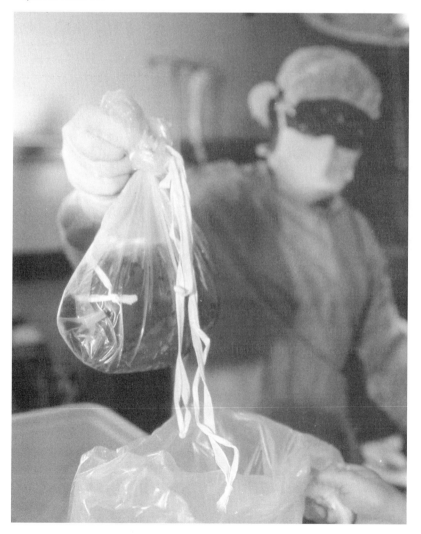

open and exposes the liver. Next, the blood vessels that supply blood to the liver are clamped shut to stop the blood flow. The old liver is removed and the donor liver is carefully put in its place. The blood vessels are connected to the new liver and then the clamps are removed, reestablishing the blood supply. Liver transplant surgery usually takes six to ten hours. A patient describes his liver transplant:

> February 16, 1996 at about 3:00 pm, I got the call. I called my wife at work and told her to get home quick to take me to the hospital. I remember racing through rush hour traffic. When I got there I was given an enema, showered and shaved. Then an IV line was put in and I was out. I remember being conscious during part of the operation. I could not open my eyes and my arms were strapped down. I could hear people talking. It wasn't very interesting so I went back to sleep. During the ten hour operation, a nurse was sent out every hour to let Alice and Mom know how I was doing.[25]

If the surgery is successful, the new liver will begin functioning as soon as the blood flow begins. According to Dr. Igal Kam, University of Colorado's Chief of Transplantation, "The most critical moment in the operation is when we release the clamps holding the blood vessels going to the new liver, and the new liver changes in color from pale or dark brown to a more pink-brown because new blood is flowing through the liver. When we see yellow-brown bile start to appear, we can relax because we know the liver is going to work. There's no room for mistakes in this procedure."[26]

Even when transplant surgery is successful, there is still a chance that the patient's immune system may reject the new liver. Since the transplanted liver is a foreign object, the immune system may attack it just as it attacks bacteria and viruses. For this reason patients are given medication, called immunosuppressants, which lower the body's ability to reject a transplanted organ by blocking the immune system's production of chemicals that attack foreign substances. Patients usually take a variety of

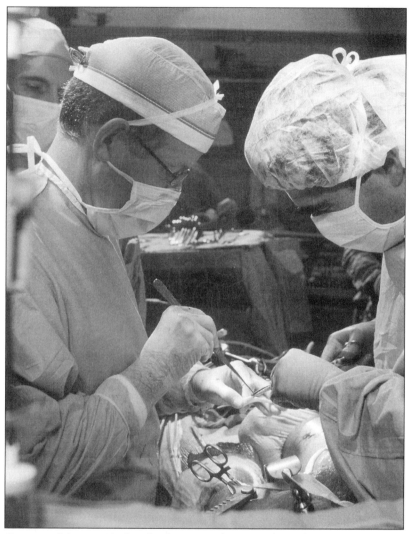

Because of the complexity of a liver transplant, a variety of specialists, known as the transplant team, are involved in the procedure.

immunosuppressants for the first three months after their transplant, since most rejections occur during this time. However, rejections can occur years later. For this reason, patients must continue taking at least one immunosuppressant all of their lives. Asked about this, a liver transplant patient explains: "Yes I have to suppress my immune system. When you transplant an organ the organ has a different DNA code. And your immune system, your white blood cells, think its an old shoe that got left in there the night the guys with knives came through. And they don't know it's your liver and its saving your life. So it wants to kick it out of your body."[27]

Even with the threat of the immune system rejecting the new liver, most liver transplants are successful; 80 to 90 percent of hepatitis patients who have liver transplants survive at least one year, and 75 to 85 percent of these patients survive for at least five years. For these patients, who otherwise are facing death, a successful liver transplant is a miracle. A hepatitis patient who had a successful liver transplant explains how it changed his life:

> I could tell the difference immediately. I am able to do many things that I enjoy. In the last year I have traveled to Washington D.C., New York, Los Angeles, San Francisco, Lake Tahoe, Vancouver B.C., Eastern Washington and the deep South. I have camped out, gone fishing, lobbied the U.S. Senate, and reached out to help as many people as possible through the Hepatitis Education project. I have a job I enjoy and work with people I like and admire. My life is good and each day is a gift.[28]

It is clear that although diagnosing hepatitis can be difficult and treatment options are limited, when treatment is effective it can change positively and even save a patient's life.

Chapter 3

Alternative Treatments

People with hepatitis have few treatment options, and more people are turning away from conventional drug treatments to alternative treatments, for several reasons. Treatment with interferon or interferon combined with ribavirin often proves to be ineffective for a large number of people. Even when interferon treatment is effective, many hepatitis patients experience very unpleasant side effects. Similarly, when interferon treatment is prescribed for asymptomatic patients, many seek alternative treatment because they are reluctant to be treated with medicine that has the potential to make them feel ill. Alternative treatments provide hepatitis patients who are unsatisfied with their treatment options other methods of containing and controlling the hepatitis virus.

A survey by the American Liver Foundation found that many hepatitis patients were more satisfied with the results of alternative treatments than they were with conventional medicine. A nonresponder who sought alternative treatment explains why she gave alternative treatments a chance:

> I was on interferon for six months and didn't respond. The interferon made me feel sicker than the hepatitis ever did. I put up with the nausea, the fever, the aches and pains, and the constant headaches because I thought the treatment would eventually clear the virus from my body, and my life would return to normal. I kept telling myself that feeling that badly was worth it, if the treatment worked. But it didn't do me

any good. My ALT levels kept going up and I still had the virus inside of me. It was very frustrating. Instead of getting better, I was deteriorating. I realized that the quality of my life is more important to me than how long I live. That's when I started looking into alternative treatments. What else could I do? I had nothing to lose.[29]

What Is Alternative Treatment?

An alternative treatment is a treatment therapy that is not widely accepted by the traditional medical community in the United States. Some forms of alternative treatments have been widely studied, while others have not. Unlike conventional treatments, which are subjected to rigorous testing before being approved by the Food and Drug Administration (FDA) for use with patients, many alternative treatments undergo only limited testing. Some alternative treatments use anecdotal evidence, or individual reports of the treatment's effectiveness, as evidence of the treatments'

These dried reishi mushrooms have positive effects on the immune system and are used as an alternative treatment for hepatitis.

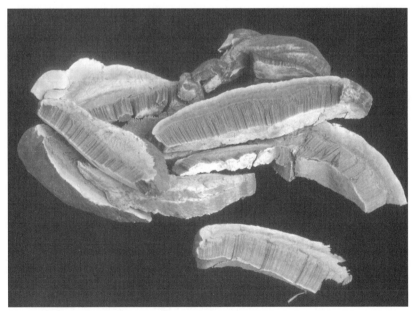

healing capabilities. Alternative treatments are not regulated by the government, and have not conclusively been proven to have a specific benefit.

Three Alternative Treatment Methods for Hepatitis

Alternative treatments for hepatitis usually fall into three categories: herbal treatments, nutritional supplements, and hormonal therapy. Of these, treatment with herbs is the most popular. Studies have shown that most people with chronic hepatitis have tried herbal treatments.

Herbal treatments are made from medicinal plants that have been used for thousands of years for healing. From medieval times until the twentieth century, when interferon treatment was developed, doctors prescribed herbal remedies as a primary treatment for hepatitis. In many parts of the globe, such as China, where one-third of all hepatitis cases in the world are currently found, herbs still are used as the main treatment for hepatitis. In fact, in an international conference on hepatitis recently held in Beijing, more than one hundred research papers were presented on the effectiveness of herbal treatments for hepatitis.

Herbal remedies used to treat disease contain leaves, stems, seeds, and roots of plants that are known to have healing properties. They are usually prescribed ground up in capsule form or as a tea. Many modern medicines are derived from herbs or consist of chemicals that are potent synthetic copies of herbs. Approximately 20 percent of all conventional prescription drugs are made by combining herbal extracts with powerful chemicals. Since herbal remedies do not use chemicals, but instead use only natural plant parts, users feel that treatment with herbs is safer and gentler than traditional chemical-based Western medicine.

Milk Thistle

The most commonly used herb to treat hepatitis is milk thistle, which currently is used throughout the world to treat all types of liver diseases. First used by the ancient Romans as a treatment for liver disease, it is one of a few herbs that has no equivalent

High levels of antioxidants are found in milk thistle, an herb that is believed to help the liver fight off damaging effects of toxins.

among traditional medications. Herbalists believe that milk thistle helps the liver to fight off the damaging effect of poisons, reduce harmful fat deposits, and regenerate. This may be due to the high level of antioxidants, or natural chemicals that fight poisons, found in milk thistle. One particular antioxidant found in milk thistle is believed to boost levels of a chemical known as glutathione, which protects the liver from damage from toxins. In addition, the seeds of the milk thistle plant contain an ingredient known as silymarin that is thought to have a wide variety of liver-strengthening effects. Herbalists theorize that when milk thistle is ingested, antioxidants help the liver fight off toxins already inside the liver. At the same time, silymarin coats and strengthens the outer membranes of the liver, blocking new toxins from entering. What's more, experts think milk thistle boosts the production of RNA, a protein used by the body to build cells, thus helping the liver to regenerate. As a result, treatment with milk thistle reduces liver inflammation and ALT levels, and slows cirrhosis.

In a study investigating milk thistle's effect on toxins in the liver, two groups of animals were given poisonous mushrooms that commonly cause liver failure. One group was also treated with milk thistle. The other group was not. The animals that were not treated with milk thistle died of liver failure, while the animals who were treated with milk thistle recovered. It appears the milk thistle blocked the poison from harming the liver, averting liver failure.

In another study, which examined milk thistle's effect on liver regeneration, two groups of rats had part of their livers removed. Again, one group was treated with milk thistle, while the other group was not. The growth of the rats' livers was monitored. More liver regeneration occurred in the rats that were given milk thistle than in the other rats.

The effect of milk thistle on humans has been widely studied in Europe. More than one hundred studies involving humans have been conducted. The results have been positive, with findings that indicate that milk thistle reduces hepatitis symptoms like fatigue, reduced appetite, and pain in the liver; and it may improve liver functions and extend the lives of patients with cirrhosis and chronic hepatitis. In 1986 the German government approved the use of milk thistle as a treatment for liver damage caused by hepatitis.

Milk thistle is usually taken in capsule form two or three times per day. It is considered most effective when 79 percent of the capsules' contents is silymarin. The mother of a child with hepatitis, who takes a number of herbs including milk thistle, describes the effects on her daughter: "Things started to improve straightaway. She started to put on weight and generally became a bright, happy and healthy child. Her blood tests have shown

Herbalists believe silymarin, an ingredient in milk thistle seeds, strengthens the liver.

continuing improvement in the past eighteen months. The change in her general health is unmistaken."[30]

The schizandra berry, a Chinese herb, is also frequently used to treat hepatitis. Although not as widely studied as milk thistle, limited studies have shown that schizandra berries help the body heal chronic hepatitis by decreasing ALT levels, which eases symptoms.

Licorice root is another herb that has not been widely studied, although it is often recommended for hepatitis. Unlike licorice candy, licorice root contains large amounts of a chemical known as glycyrrhizic acid that appears to lessen liver inflammation. Herbalists think it does this by prompting the body to produce interferon.

Mixing these and other herbs, which have various properties thought to lower inflammation, strengthen the liver, or decrease hepatitis symptoms, is another way herbs are frequently used to treat hepatitis. Many Chinese herbal treatments follow this method. Bing gan ling, for example, is a mix of various plants and roots traditionally used to treat hepatitis in China. Chinese studies showed that this mixture significantly lowers ALT levels. According to hepatitis specialist Dr. Keivan Jinnah, "I find that Chinese herbal formulas, which contain anywhere from eight to fifteen different herbs to be the most effective treatment for Hep C. The Chinese herbs are capable of stopping the process of destruction that is taking place in the liver, and I believe, reverse it."[31]

Nutritional Supplements

The second most popular type of alternative treatment used for hepatitis is nutritional supplements, such as vitamins and minerals, that are used to augment nutritional deficiencies caused by liver problems and to help fight off the hepatitis virus. Vitamin B complex, vitamin C, vitamin E, vitamin K, zinc, calcium, cobalt, and manganese are among the vitamins and minerals most commonly prescribed. Many of these vitamins act as antioxidants. They prevent poisons found in drugs, alcohol, pollution, and cigarette smoke from entering the liver where they cause scar tissue to form, which worsens cirrhosis. Many patients take antioxidant cocktails, in which large doses of vitamin B complex, vitamin C, and vitamin E are combined, in an effort to strengthen their livers. A patient who uses nutritional supplements talks about how they have helped her: "I take a mix of anti-oxidants and minerals three times a day. Since I started, there's been a big difference in how I feel. My energy level is up and I feel a lot stronger. My ALT levels are the best they've been in years. Things seem to be looking up. I feel like I can start planning for the future. I'm optimistic I'll live to see it."[32]

Hormonal Therapy

The third form of alternative treatment, hormonal therapy, involves the use of chemicals produced by the thymus gland, a small gland in the chest that manufactures white blood cells and

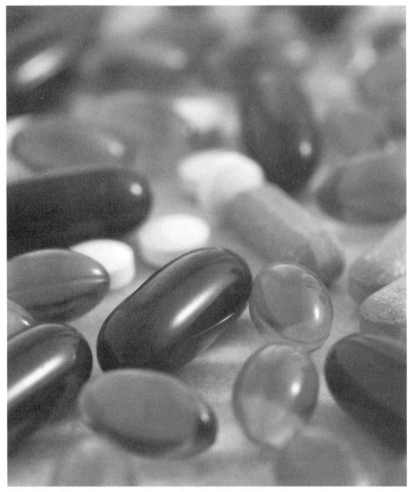

Nutritional supplements such as vitamins B and E can boost the energy levels of hepatitis patients.

naturally makes interferon during childhood. However, the thymus gland shrinks and ceases functioning as people grow older. Although many scientists believe that adults no longer need the chemicals produced by the thymus gland, believers in hormonal therapy think this chemical is necessary for the immune system to fight off the hepatitis virus. Consequently, patients take a combination of thymic chemicals, or enzymes, that are derived from the thymus gland of cows as a way to replace the infection-fighting ability of the shrunken thymus gland. Thymic therapy is usually prescribed in injection form as well as in capsules and is frequently combined with nutritional supplements. Studies into the effectiveness of this therapy are inconclusive. Some studies have found thymic therapy to be ineffective, while other studies have produced more positive results. According to Dr. Carson Burgstiner, who developed thymic therapy in 1983 to treat his own hepatitis and then used it to treat his patients,

> The results have been dramatic! Ninety percent of the hepatitis B cases have been arrested in six weeks and most hepatitis C cases within three months. Other exciting progress with the use of the thymic formula and vitamin-mineral complex supplements involve three transplant patients. These individuals were scheduled to have liver transplants and are no longer on transplant lists having recovered from chronic hepatitis.[33]

Unconventional Treatment Methods

Many of these alternative treatments appear to offer patients relief, but the effectiveness and safety of others are more controversial. Among the most controversial treatments are those that claim to be based on "secret" formulas that claim to protect, strengthen, detoxify, and regenerate the liver. Others claim to get rid of the hepatitis virus, which is unlikely. Such controversial methods often use "mysterious" or questionable ingredients or unconventional methods. Urine therapy is one such controversial treatment. It involves the drinking of a small amount of one's own urine each day. Developed in India thousands of years ago, this therapy is based on the theory that the proteins and chemicals found in urine can detoxify the liver and promote healing and long life. Since urine is actually a form of filtered blood produced by the kidneys, this therapy is not dangerous. However, there is little proof of its effectiveness.

Bloodletting is another unconventional therapy that employs a questionable method of treatment. Bloodletting involves the use of leeches or special metal instruments that are used to drain a prescribed amount of a patient's blood. Bloodletting was originally used in medieval times as a way to remove poisons from the blood. Today bloodletting is believed to reduce the level of iron in the liver, which, when it exceeds certain levels, may accelerate the progress of liver damage. After blood is removed, special medicinal creams often are placed on the bleeding points to intensify the effect. Although excess iron can harm people with hepatitis, there is little proof of the effectiveness of this method and excessive bloodletting can cause weakness and fatigue.

Since there are so many alternative treatments and the effectiveness of some are controversial, the American Liver Foundation advises patients to consult with their doctors who can help them evaluate which treatments are best and help them find reputable alternative health care products and practitioners. In addition to consulting their physicians, patients can find reliable information about alternative treatments in a variety of sources. Although there is no regulatory agency in the United States that recommends herbal treatments, patients can get valuable information from an agency regulated by the German government known as Commission E. Commission E assesses and regulates herbal treatments in Germany. It reports on the effectiveness of hundreds of herbs each year. *The Physicians Desk Reference for Herbal Medicines,* a manual that provides information about more than three hundred herbs, is another good source of information, as is the National Institute of Health's Division of Alternative Medicine, which documents the results of research on alternative treatments.

Doctors can also help patients combine traditional treatment with alternative treatments in a method known as integrative treatment. This therapy combines interferon with an herbal treatment, or interferon with nutritional supplements. Hepatitis specialist Dr. Bruce Bacon discusses how he uses integrative treatment:

> My approach to this is that if I've made a decision someone should be treated, I want to do whatever is possible to get them through the course of treatment. So if getting someone

through treatment involves them using alternative or integrative forms of medicine to help them deal with the disease, I'm all for it. I support my patients to do that. I think a lot of the use of alternative medicines and integrative forms of therapy provide patients with the opportunity to still be, at least in part, in control of what they're doing. I think that's healthy, and that's good.[34]

Risks and Side Effects of Alternative Medicines

Although many patients turn to alternative treatments hoping to find gentler and more effective forms of treatment, they also are exposing themselves to potentially serious health risks. Although alternative treatments may improve the patients' symptoms,

Although alternative treatments can ease the symptoms of hepatitis, they cannot rid cells of the virus (shown below).

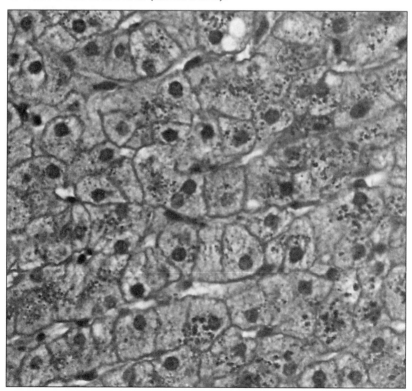

most experts believe that they cannot eliminate the hepatitis virus or the damage it causes. Nor can alternative treatments replace a lifesaving liver transplant. One of the greatest risks occurs when patients opt for alternative treatments instead of interferon treatment or a liver transplant.

Lack of regulations of alternative products also presents health hazards, and problems may arise from the use of herbs, nutritional supplements, and hormones. Lack of set dosages complicates treatment with these substances. Unlike the monitoring of conventional medicine, in which government agencies supervise the level of active ingredients, levels of active ingredients in herbs, nutritional supplements, and hormones are not monitored, even when the ingredients may be as powerful as those found in prescription drugs. Many patients, unaware of this, assume that because they are natural, these products are safe. However, this is not always correct. Herbs, nutritional supplements, and hormones may be too strong, causing a bad reaction. In fact, there have been cases in which the strength of herbal products has been found to be three times the amount stated on the label. High doses of certain herbs can cause vomiting, heart problems, strokes, and even paralysis. Patients are just as likely to have an allergic reaction to herbs and supplements as they are to drugs. Due to the absence of regulations, the product may contain totally different herbs than those listed on the label. Herbs that are mixed with products that are harmful to the liver, such as tranquilizers, painkillers, and steroids, have also been marketed. Even widely used treatments such as milk thistle pose risks. Hepatitis expert Dr. Alan Berkman discusses the dangers of this herb: "There are no clinical trials to suggest which patients it might work for; there are no regulations concerning its purity or concentration, which may vary considerably from one batch to another; no one knows the proper dosage quantities; and there is no knowledge of its side effects, drug interactions, or other possible dangers."[35]

Experts speculate that the very qualities in silymarin that help it detoxify the liver also may keep the liver from absorbing other medications the patient may be taking, rendering them ineffective. Patients also have reported skin rashes, headaches, irritability, and serious stomach upset as a result of taking milk thistle. Moreover, the long-term side effects of alternative treatments are still unknown. Other problems such as fluid retention, which causes patients to swell up, are reported as a side effect of licorice. This can be particularly troubling for many hepatitis patients who already may be suffering from fluid retention as a result of the liver malfunctioning. Licorice also may cause high blood pressure, a dangerous condition that can lead to strokes.

Other herbs commonly found in herbal mixtures can have grave effects on patients' livers. Since every food or drink, including herbal teas and capsules, that enters the body is broken down by the liver, the liver is especially vulnerable to the toxic

The herb chapparal can be dangerous to the liver, causing unpredictable side effects especially when mixed with other herbs.

effects of herbs. Experts agree that when herbs are mixed, they frequently can produce unpredictable side effects. Combinations of herbs containing Asian ginseng, comfrey, hops, coltsfoot, chaparral, valerian, pennyroyal, and germander are especially dangerous. These herbs have been reported to cause serious liver damage, and, at high doses, liver poisoning. Germander, in particular, is considered so toxic to the liver that it is banned in France. Similarly, use of chaparral is reported to be so hazardous that it has been known to cause liver failure. A patient who experienced problems when she mixed herbs describes her experience:

> I went to a health food store and asked them to give me anything that would help my liver. I got coltsfoot, comfrey, petasites, chaparral and yohimbe. My enzymes shot up to 800. When the doctor asked me if I was taking anything new, I brought in the bottles and learned that these herbs were best avoided because they may be toxic for the liver. I stopped taking them and my enzymes went back down. I never thought anything natural could harm me.[36]

Megadoses of vitamins and minerals can also damage the liver. Large doses of vitamins such as vitamin A, vitamin D, and vitamin K, which cannot be cleared from the body in urine and, as a result, build up to dangerous amounts in the liver, can cause severe liver damage. Excessive doses of vitamin A, in particular, can cause a liver disease known as hypervitaminosis A, which can result in high blood pressure and cirrhosis. Even small doses of these vitamins may harm the liver. Symptoms include nausea, headache, depression, hair loss, dry skin, and constant thirst. Iron, a mineral found in many multiple vitamins, can also cause severe damage to the liver. Excess iron cannot be eliminated from the liver, and may actually cause or worsen liver cell damage and cirrhosis and lead to liver cancer. Experts theorize that when excess iron builds up in the liver, increased liver cell mutation may occur raising the risk of liver cancer.

Although the FDA does not study the effectiveness of herbs or nutritional supplements, after these products are on the market this agency does have the responsibility of warning the public if a product is unsafe. As a result, the FDA has issued a list of herbs and supplements that are associated with liver illness or injury. This list includes chaparral, comfrey, germander, vitamin A, and the mineral niacin.

Despite these possible health risks, millions of desperate people with hepatitis who have found conventional drug treatments ineffective turn to alternative treatment in hopes of avoiding liver failure. "When the interferon didn't work, I felt desperate," a chronic hepatitis patient who turned to alternative treatments explains. "At best, all I had to look forward to was severe liver damage or a liver transplant, and at worst, an early death, not the best options. But if this [alternative] treatment works and it seems to be, I can live a normal life."[37]

Chapter 4

Living with Hepatitis

Daily life can be a challenge for people with chronic hepatitis. They must cope with both physical and emotional challenges that impact not only their own lives, but also the lives of their loved ones. If these challenges are not met, hepatitis patients risk the threat of liver failure, and their loved ones risk the threat of contracting the virus. Often, the best way for hepatitis patients to face these challenges successfully involves making a number of changes in their daily life.

Physical Challenges

Chronic fatigue, characterized by long-term feelings of weakness and exhaustion, is a frequent complaint of many hepatitis patients. Experts are unsure why chronic fatigue troubles hepatitis patients. Some theorize that ongoing liver injury causes the liver to release, rather than filter out, waste products into the bloodstream, which weaken the patient. Others speculate that the hepatitis virus itself and the immune system's attempt to fight it weaken the body, causing chronic fatigue. Worsening matters, patients receiving interferon treatment commonly suffer from chronic fatigue as a side effect of their treatment.

No matter what the cause is, chronic fatigue causes hepatitis patients to have so little stamina that even performing small tasks becomes difficult. Due to extreme drops in their energy levels, people facing this challenge often find themselves overcome by exhaustion. This lack of energy can be so debilitating that many people have to reduce or eliminate many normal activities. A patient describes this fatigue as, "Feeling as though I have been laid out by a professional boxer. It often comes on suddenly and means I have to stop everything I am doing immediately and go and lie down. I think that people sometimes think I am just tired, when in fact I am completely incapable of any activity whatsoever."[38]

Another physical challenge is loss of appetite and resulting weight loss. Symptoms of hepatitis and the effects of interferon can cause loss of appetite and nausea. Interferon treatment often causes patients to develop a bad taste in their mouths, and liver disease can affect the way a person reacts to different tastes. As a result, many patients find that certain foods no longer taste good to them. Complicating matters, when the liver is inflamed it often presses against the stomach making sufferers feel that there is little room for food inside of them, which further reduces their appetites. All of these factors, combined with liver damage, which decreases the liver's ability to store and distribute nutrients, make it hard for hepatitis patients to keep weight on and may result in malnutrition. "I had a lot of muscle because I was a physical therapist," a hepatitis patient who is dealing with this challenge reports. "When I look in the mirror now, I can see the wasting. I'm so much thinner in my arms, shoulders and back."[39]

Fluid retention is another physical challenge that many hepatitis patients must cope with. This happens when scarred liver cells are no longer able to adequately filter waste from the bloodstream. When this occurs, the body loses its ability to eliminate excess salt and water. As a result, patients must deal with unpleasant swelling of different parts of the body. According to Dr. Gregory Everson, "Liver disease generates signals to the kidney to retain both salt and water. The salt acts like a sponge. As a result, fluid accumulates in certain tissues and body spaces, such as the ankles, abdomen and chest."[40]

Still another challenge caused by the liver's inability to filter waste products from the blood is itching, which occurs when waste products build up under the skin. Unlike itchiness caused by a rash or insect bite, this itching is neither temporary,

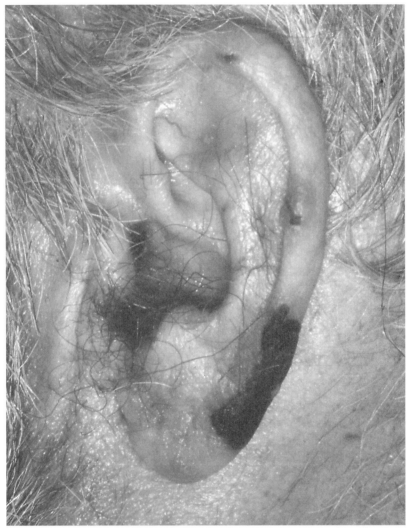

When the liver can no longer filter waste from the blood a rash develops on the skin and patients experience chronic itchiness.

nor easily relieved. A hepatitis patient talks about this challenge: "It began as a little itch. I hardly noticed it. I ignored it until it got bigger, and I started scratching. There was one spot the size of a quarter on my left leg. Creams did no good. Over a year-and-a-half, it got so bad I swore I'd never scratch—and I've got high will power. But I scarred my leg."[41]

Emotional Challenges

People with hepatitis also face a variety of emotional challenges. Hepatitis patients often feel ashamed when people do not treat them with sympathy because of the way they contracted the disease. A patient explains how this has affected her: "The mere mention to someone that I probably acquired Hepatitis C through IV drug use is met with a certain demeanor of repugnance. It is like I get pushed back twenty years over and over. No matter what I'm like today, it doesn't seem to make a difference. I really want people to get a different view of hepatitis sufferers. No matter how we contracted this deadly virus, we deserve respect."[42]

Feelings of shame and anger may also result when a patient's peers do not understand properly the way hepatitis is spread, and simply avoid all contact with them. According to one patient, "When I tell someone I have hepatitis the atmosphere changes. I've had people give me the airbrush handshake because they don't want to touch me. Suddenly, there's this invisible wall."[43]

People with hepatitis also must cope with fear of spreading the disease to their loved ones. Patients in long-term monogamous sexual relationships must confront the risk of spreading hepatitis to their mates. Sometimes this threat leads to divorce. Single people must tell partners about their disease before starting an intimate relationship, which frequently results in rejection. As one patient explains: "Before my diagnosis, I was seeing a man I knew I could get serious about. I panicked about how and when to tell him that I had a communicable disease and felt a mounting sense of dread at the prospect. We have since gone our separate ways and hepatitis definitely played a part in our difficulties. It was one thing for him to say he accepted my disease, but another to live with the challenge and threat of it."[44]

These emotional challenges often cause hepatitis patients to feel isolated. Depression, which can decrease a person's ability to concentrate, increase fatigue and pain, and cause irritability and sudden outbursts of temper, may result. Research directed by the Veterans Affairs Medical Center found abnormally high numbers of hepatitis patients suffering from depression.

Scientists acknowledge that there may be a physical link between depression and hepatitis. One theory is that when the liver is damaged, levels of chemicals normally produced and regulated by the liver become unbalanced, resulting in depression. Side effects of interferon also may lead to depression. Since it takes three years for all traces of interferon to be cleared from the body, depression can occur years after treatment. Poor blood circulation to the brain resulting from liver damage and interferon therapy may also cause depression.

No matter what causes people with hepatitis to develop depression, depression can weaken the immune system and diminish the body's ability to fight off the hepatitis virus, which can result in further liver damage. Another consequence of depression is the development of irritability. Some researchers think this is due to the damaged liver's inability to regulate and break down substances produced by the body, called hormones, which may lead patients to have uncontrollable explosions of temper and unexplained irritability. A patient discusses how this has affected him: "I am starting to get impatient with people and my tolerance level has dropped. This is totally out of character for me. I think that this all may be related to depression."[45]

Overcoming Obstacles

Despite these challenges most people with hepatitis lead happy and productive lives. The key, patients and experts agree, is maintaining a balance between doing things to keep their livers healthy while they keep from spreading the disease to others. This frequently involves people with hepatitis making a number of changes in their lives. According to one patient, "Having chronic hepatitis C is a major issue for me in life and in recovery. It is very real in my life and affects how I live to a large extent. I have had to be willing to change many things: how I work; how I play; how I rest; what I eat; who I have in my life; and most importantly, my expectations of myself."[46]

Ways Hepatitis Patients Can Stay Healthy

- **Follow a low-fat diet**

- **Limit protein intake**

- **Eat complex carbohydrates**

- **Limit sodium intake**

- **Avoid alcohol**

- **Avoid smoking**

Maintenance and Monitoring

One of the most important things people with hepatitis do to keep their liver healthy is to follow a liver-healthy diet, which frequently requires patients to make a number of changes in their diets. According to Dr. Melissa Palmer,

> Everything that enters the body must pass through the liver to be processed. The liver is responsible for the production and use of most nutrients. Therefore, everything that is ingested has an effect on the liver—some positive, some negative. That's why it is advisable for people to eat foods with an eye towards promoting liver health. Most people with liver disease need to restrict some foods from their diets. This should not be viewed as a punishment, but rather a step in the direction of a healthier liver.[47]

The liver is important in breaking down and distributing protein, carbohydrates, and fats used by the body for energy and strength. When the liver is fighting the hepatitis virus and, consequently, is not functioning properly, it cannot efficiently break down and distribute these nutrients, resulting in a lack of energy.

Therefore, it is very important for hepatitis patients to eat foods that maximize energy and put limited stress on the liver, making its job easier. This includes the limiting of fat, protein, and simple carbohydrates.

Excess fat and protein can build up in hepatitis patients' livers. Fat deposits can cause rapid scarring of the liver to occur, while excessive protein can cause a condition known as encephalopathy, which causes drowsiness and mental confusion. For this reason, fat and protein intake is frequently restricted. A patient explains why he is limiting protein in his diet: "While I was waiting for my liver transplant, I'd get in the car and forget if I was leaving or coming. If you've got too much protein, it can cause you to fall asleep at the intersection. The doctor told me to stop driving and put me on a protein-restricted diet. I watch the amount I take in, and if I feel too tired, I cut back."[48]

Similarly, carbohydrates are processed by the liver and stored as a chemical known as glycogen, which the liver releases into the blood in a steady stream in order to provide the body with energy. When the liver is damaged it cannot store or release simple carbohydrates found in sugar, candy, cakes, and other pastries efficiently. However, even a damaged liver can process and release complex carbohydrates found in fruits, vegetables, bread, cereal, pasta, and rice at a constant level, boosting energy. For this reason, people with hepatitis are advised to limit their intake of simple carbohydrates while raising their intake of complex carbohydrates. "Yes, it's true, I used to be a junk food junkie," a patient who made this change explains. "I was always eating chips and candy bars, and I was always tired. The doctor told me that I had to be kinder to my liver. So I switched to eating more complex carbohydrates like fruits and vegetables. Yes, I miss the sweets, but I have a lot more energy."[49]

Since the hepatitis virus multiplies more rapidly when iron is present, people with hepatitis often must limit their dietary intake of iron. Sodium, or salt, is also frequently restricted because too much sodium can increase fluid retention. A patient who faced this challenge explains: "The dietician restricted me to 2000

Patients with hepatitis must control their diet by eating more complex carbohydrates and fewer iron-rich foods.

milligrams of sodium a day. That's one teaspoon! I try, but I really like salt. If I don't watch carefully though—say I eat some broth, and it has salt in it—I pick up extra water. Once I had thirty pounds of water on me. I had a belly like a pregnant rhino. My wife says if I wouldn't cover everything with 'white death', I'd do a lot better."[50] Because of this problem some hepatitis patients must take a diuretic, a medication that helps the body eliminate excess fluids.

Hepatitis patients with liver damage must be cautious of sugary foods such as these pastries.

Another dietary change that helps hepatitis patients' livers to function better and provides patients with more energy is eating more frequent, smaller meals. This is important because a damaged liver often is unable to process large amounts of nutrients at one time, resulting in low energy levels. Smaller, more frequent meals put less strain on the liver while providing the body with more energy. In addition, since many hepatitis patients suffer from poor appetite, eating more but smaller meals is less over-whelming and helps prevent weight loss.

Frequent medical monitoring is another important way people with hepatitis help keep their liver healthy. Threatened by pro-gressive liver disease, and the numerous side effects of interferon therapy, hepatitis patients must undergo periodic medical exams and blood tests that monitor their condition by tracking their vi-ral and ALT levels. Such tests warn of any changes in the liver. Many patients have liver biopsies every three or four years in or-der to monitor their liver even more closely.

Lifestyle Changes

Besides changing their diet and receiving frequent medical mon-itoring, people with hepatitis must kick personal habits like smoking or drinking alcohol. Alcohol, like all other drugs and toxins, is filtered out of the blood and sent to the liver to be neu-tralized. Due to the high levels of iron found in most alcoholic drinks, once inside the liver, alcohol causes the hepatitis virus to multiply rapidly, accelerating the progress of the disease. Studies have shown that hepatitis patients who drink are more likely to develop cirrhosis and have a 25 percent greater chance of devel-oping liver cancer than hepatitis patients who do not drink. Ex-perts theorize that by avoiding alcohol, people with hepatitis reduce stress on their livers and prevent additional damage to healthy liver cells. A patient explains why she avoids alcohol: "I have made many changes in my life since my diagnosis, the toughest being giving up alcohol. In deference to my liver, I try not to drink. The less work my liver has to do, including filtering any toxins I put into my body, the better."[51]

Similarly, people with hepatitis must refrain from smoking. Like alcohol, nicotine is a toxin that the liver must remove from the bloodstream. This is a difficult task for a damaged liver. As a result, nicotine remains in the body causing problems such as poor circulation and poor lung health. Experts theorize that smoking also depletes the body's supply of vitamin C, which is needed by the immune system to fight disease. Therefore, smok-ing makes it harder for the immune system to battle the hepatitis

The presence of alcohol in the liver causes the hepatitis virus to multiply rapidly.

virus, and it accelerates the progress of the disease. Smoking has also been linked to the development of liver cancer in hepatitis patients. According to Dr. Melissa Palmer, "Smoking may diminish the liver's ability to detoxify dangerous substances. Cigarettes may worsen the course of liver disease. Cigarettes have been associated with a possible increased incidence of liver cancer. Therefore, people with liver disease should refrain from cigarette smoking."[52]

People with hepatitis must also use caution when using over-the-counter medicines. Since the liver processes all medications, hepatitis patients must be aware of which drugs are difficult for the liver to detoxify and avoid these medicines. For example, acetaminophen, a common painkiller found in Tylenol, can be

Smoking puts hepatitis patients at high risk for developing liver cancer.

highly toxic to hepatitis patients' livers. Acetaminophen can cause severe liver damage, even liver failure, and therefore must be avoided.

Protecting Others

In addition to coping with the effects of hepatitis and living a liver-healthy life, people with hepatitis must take steps to keep from infecting others. Since hepatitis is spread through blood, people with hepatitis can protect others by covering cuts and open sores, by being careful to clean all bloodstains, including menstrual blood, with disinfectant, and by refusing to donate blood or be a tissue donor. People with hepatitis should identify themselves as hepatitis patients to all their health care providers such as doctors, nurses, laboratory technicians, and dentists, so these professionals can take proper precautions. Patients should not share any type of needles or personal items that can carry virus-laden blood, such as earrings, razors, or toothbrushes. In addition, people with hepatitis should discuss their disease with their sexual partners, and should practice safe sex. Hepatitis patients and experts agree that it is very important that people with hepatitis educate themselves so they know how the disease is spread, and what is or is not safe to do. Knowing that the disease is not spread through casual contact frees people with hepatitis to do normal things like hugging, kissing, and shaking hands without fear. This helps them to maintain balance in their lives. A young mother with hepatitis explains how important this understanding is: "I was so scared at first that I would give it to someone else. I didn't even want to hold a baby. When you first find out you're grasping for answers. Am I contagious? That's why it's very important for you to become educated about the virus. The biggest challenge is to keep living your life and to not let your illness take over."[53]

Coping

Although dealing with these challenges can be difficult, people with hepatitis use a number of strategies to help them cope and enjoy their lives. Among these strategies is participating in support groups. Hepatitis support groups are made up of people with hepatitis who share their experiences. These groups give members a chance to share their feelings while providing information, encouragement, and a sense of belonging. By sharing their common experiences support group members often find solutions to problems that people without hepatitis do not understand. A hepatitis patient who was having trouble coping explains how joining a support group helped her: "The turning point may have come for me when I became involved in the

Hepatitis patients should strive for a healthy lifestyle that includes physical fitness.

Experts believe that meditation can help the hepatitis patient relax and focus on healing their bodies.

support group, which has empowered me, informed me, and given me a focus. I would recommend that everyone gets involved in some kind of self-help group. If twenty people have the same symptoms, twenty times the symptoms means twenty ways of dealing with them!"[54]

Moderate exercise also helps people with hepatitis cope.

Studies have shown that physical activity strengthens the body and also improves the exerciser's emotional state. Exercise increases blood circulation, which may help prevent or lessen the effects of cirrhosis and prevent depression. It helps eliminate fatigue and has been linked to improving the immune system, which helps the body fight the hepatitis virus. It also counteracts stress, which is dangerous to the immune system. According to Dr. Melissa Palmer, "Regular exercise is an important component necessary to combat liver disease. People who exercise on a regular basis not only feel better, but often respond more positively to medical treatment. Regular exercise will increase energy levels, decrease stress on the liver, and, in many cases, even delay the onset of certain complications associated with liver disease."[55]

Meditation and guided imagery are other methods many hepatitis patients use to keep their livers healthy. Meditation involves using concentration techniques such as silently repeating a word or sound to quiet the mind. While meditating, people focus on a word or phrase in order to wipe all thoughts from their mind and relax their bodies. Many experts believe that meditation helps to strengthen the immune system by relieving stress. Guided imagery is a form of meditation in which people focus their thoughts on relaxing and healing their bodies. Many hepatitis patients use guided imagery to imagine their immune systems fighting and defeating the hepatitis virus. "Every night that was a shot night," a patient who used guided imagery to boost interferon therapy explains, "I would go into a guided imagery practice as I was injecting the interferon. I imagined that I had completely cleared the virus from my body, that there was crystal clear water rinsing all the inflammation and dead viral cells from my liver. I completely believe that these practices helped my body respond to the interferon. It certainly helped me live in the moment and make the best use of my experience."[56]

Although living with hepatitis can be challenging, most people with hepatitis make the best of their experience. They make changes in their lives in order to keep their livers healthy and avoid spreading the disease to others. This helps them to live happy and productive lives. As a patient who has met these challenges explains: "Yes, I have hepatitis. Yes, I'm careful about what I eat and drink. Yes, I'm mindful of protecting my loved ones. But that is only part of my life. I have a wonderful family, great friends and a job I enjoy. I'm proud of who I am, and how I'm taking care of myself, and I enjoy being alive, every single day."[57]

Chapter 5

What the Future Holds

In order to learn more about hepatitis, scientists throughout the world are conducting a wide range of studies. More than $34 million per year is being spent on hepatitis research in the hope that the results will provide people with hepatitis a better quality of life in the future.

Improving Treatments

Unlike treatments for other diseases, where a variety of drugs are readily available for patients who don't respond to one particular medication, treatment for hepatitis is limited to interferon, which is often ineffective and causes many serious side effects. Making matters worse, when a liver transplant is necessary, many people with hepatitis die before a compatible liver can be found due to the shortage of available livers. Because of the urgency of these factors, scientists are focusing most hepatitis research on developing more effective treatments. They are concentrating on learning more about the viruses that cause hepatitis, how the viruses affect the liver, and the liver, itself.

A Difficult Task

The primary goal of all hepatitis research is the development of a potent vaccine like that for hepatitis A and B, which would prevent or cure hepatitis C. Scientists have been trying to create such a vaccine for over a decade, but little progress has been made. The task is so complex that scientists at the National Institute of Allergy and Infectious Diseases predict the development of such

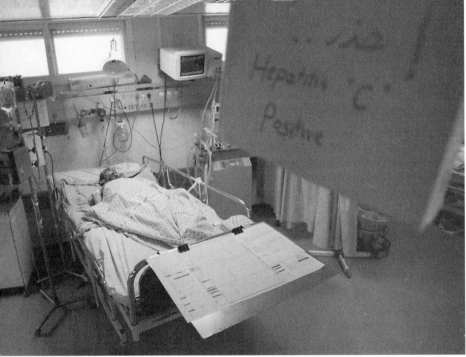

A patient is hospitalized for hepatitis C, which rapidly multiplies and mutates in the body.

a vaccine will not occur for at least another ten years. During this time many hepatitis patients may face serious liver damage, which is the reason that most research is concentrating on creating more effective treatments now.

The problem scientists face in developing a vaccine is caused by the rapid rate in which the hepatitis C virus multiplies and mutates. Researchers theorize that one hepatitis C virus can produce more than 150 different subtypes or mutations, and each subtype can produce about twenty other different mutations, which also mutate, and so on. As a result, people with hepatitis C may have over a trillion different hepatitis virus particles in their bodies. Because of this, a vaccine developed to cripple the original virus would be ineffective against its mutations. According to experts at the Hepatitis Information Network, "Hepatitis C mutates even more than hepatitis B. So much so, in fact, that the body ends up having to fight many, many slightly different forms or strains of hepatitis C. This has made producing a vaccine for hepatitis C difficult. A vaccine against the virus would probably need to protect against many strains at once or you would need several vaccines."[58]

Producing a single vaccine against hepatitis C is a complex task because of the various strains of the virus.

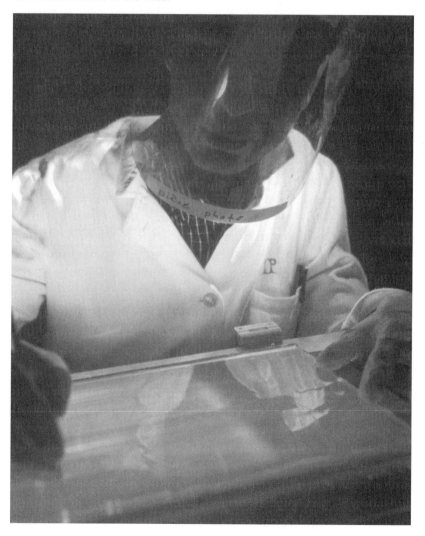

One way scientists are hoping to overcome this problem is by trying to identify how the virus enters the host cells. Scientists hypothesize that since the hepatitis virus is found only in the liver and does not target any other organs, every mutation of the virus must have a common chemical or mechanism that allows it to enter the liver. Through continued study they hope to identify this common feature and then develop a vaccine that targets it, crippling the virus's access to the liver. However, progress in this area has been slow because not enough is currently known about the virus. Consequently, scientists are studying the virus and the liver hoping to develop new and better treatments that can help patients right now. Researchers anticipate that through these studies they will gain enough knowledge about the virus to speed up the development of a vaccine.

Learning About the Virus

In order to learn more about the virus, a major focus of research has been attempts to artificially grow the hepatitis virus in a laboratory. Scientists have met with some success in doing this. In 1997 Food and Drug Administration researchers successfully cloned a hepatitis C virus. Then in 1999 German researchers produced the first man-made hepatitis C virus. However, keeping these artificially grown viruses alive long enough to study them has proven difficult. Consequently, a number of current studies are focusing on developing a cell culture of the hepatitis virus in order to examine its life cycle. By closely observing the life cycle of the virus, scientists hope to gain information about how the virus forms, multiplies, mutates, injures cells, and enters the bloodstream. They believe that understanding this process will lead to the development of a variety of medications that will block the different parts of the virus's life cycle. According to Dr. Gregory Everson, "Understanding these critical steps required to maintain the infection will allow scientists to develop medications or strategies to stop the virus from reproducing and, ultimately, to eradicate the infection."[59]

In studying the virus's life cycle, many scientists are trying to learn more about how the virus reproduces and mutates. By reproducing, the virus sustains the infection. Therefore, if the virus could be kept from reproducing, it eventually would die out. Consequently, ongoing research is concentrating on developing drugs that block reproduction. Two antiviral drugs known as adefovir and lobucavir currently are being tested. These medications closely resemble a part of the hepatitis virus that contains the proteins DNA and RNA, which are part of a chain of substances that the virus needs to reproduce. Because of this resemblance, scientists theorize that the virus mistakes the adefovir and lobucavir for DNA and RNA and unsuccessfully tries to use the drugs to make copies of itself, which interrupts the chain and blocks reproduction. Tests with these drugs done on human volunteers, known as clinical trials, have been promising. In one clinical trial, the viral levels of two-thirds of the patients treated for hepatitis B with adefovir were lowered by 99 percent. Adefovir also seems to work on viral mutations that have proven resistant to other drugs. As research director Alison Murray explains: "Adefovir is effective against resistant virus strains. The drug molecules resemble building blocks of DNA and RNA, except they are missing a crucial side chain. As the drug seeps into all the cells of the liver, viruses pick it up and try to use it to construct copies of themselves. Without the critical link, however, the virus cannot attach the other blocks onto the drug, and the viral assembly line shuts down."[60]

Other studies are focusing on how the hepatitis virus mutates. Studies conducted by the National Institute of Allergy and Infectious Diseases have found that the virus does not mutate at the same rate in every person. These studies found that when the virus mutates more slowly, patients are more likely to clear the virus out of their systems than are people in whom the virus changes rapidly. Scientists speculate that this is because the immune systems of the patients with the slower mutating viruses have fewer varieties of the virus to fight against. In addition, some mutated forms of the virus appear to develop a protein on their surface that allows them to hide from white blood cells sent by the immune system to destroy them. On the

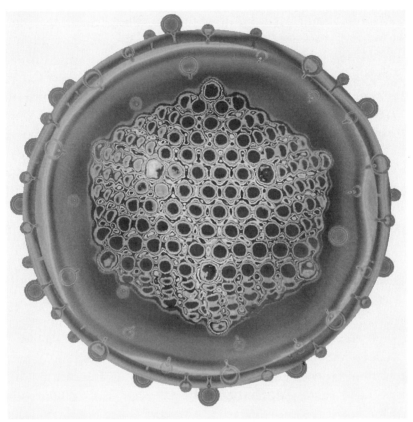

This model of hepatitis A is used to test antiviral drugs that will contain proteins that resemble the virus's own RNA and DNA.

other hand, the patients in whom the virus mutates the fastest are more likely to develop chronic forms of hepatitis and become nonresponders. Scientists theorize that this occurs because certain mutations or subtypes of the virus are able to elude the immune system, and simultaneously resist or block the effects of interferon and eliminate it rapidly from the body.

Using this knowledge, scientists have been developing new medications that they hope will overpower these resistant viruses. Among these medications is a new form of pegylated interferon, known as peginterferon. Peginterferon is covered with a layer of chemicals that, scientists think, helps keep it from being resisted and eliminated from the body by the mutated virus. As a result, peginterferon stays in the body longer, increasing the virus's exposure to the drug. It also seems to have less troubling side effects than interferon. Results of a number of clinical trials, where peginterferon was used alone and in combination with ribivirin, have been quite promising. In fact, in one clinical trial where peginterferon and ribivirin were combined, 54 percent of the patients were responders and had undetectable levels of the hepatitis virus in their blood six months after the treatment had ended. This is a record number. According to researcher Dr. Michael Fried of the University of North Carolina, "We are pleased with this impressive response in those treated with PEG interferon combination. The bottom line is that we now have a highly effective therapy that many patients can tolerate. The results of this trial are welcome news to physicians and certainly to patients."[61]

A patient who participated in a clinical trial that used peginterferon, which appears to have cleared all traces of the virus from her system, talks about her experience: "I got real nauseated. I was tired. I didn't have any reserve energy. But when you know there's a chance for a cure, it is worth it. If I had to do it over again, I'd do it. Now I am back at full steam. Nobody could be more thrilled than I am."[62]

Another area of research aimed at combating the mutated virus's ability to resist interferon is the development of a wide combination of different drugs, which may include combining interferon or peginterferon with a large number of other medications that are used to bombard the virus. Scientists theorize that this barrage of multiple antiviral medications should cripple the virus, making it impossible for it to develop enough mutations fast enough to resist the effects of all the drugs. This type of treatment currently is being used successfully to treat HIV that causes AIDS. A clinical trial using this treatment for hepatitis had promising results, and researchers are currently developing a variety of new antiviral drugs to use in this mix. According to E. Jenny Heathcote, a professor of medicine at the University of Toronto, who is involved in these studies, "I am not convinced that any patient with hepatitis should be treated with a single agent. It's like many years ago when we were trying to treat HIV with just AZT. In retrospect we realized that we should have been using cocktails (of several agents), because the virus becomes resistant so quickly to just one drug."[63]

The development of new antiviral drugs for combination treatment and studies into how the hepatitis virus reproduces has led to the development of another form of treatment known as protease inhibitors. Using computer-based technology to analyze the structure of the hepatitis virus, researchers have found that the hepatitis virus contains a chemical known as protease, which it uses in the reproductive chain to produce infectious copies of itself. Although the virus can replicate without protease, the mutations cannot infect other cells. Scientists currently are developing protease inhibitors to attach to and block the part of the virus that contains protease, making it impossible for protease to be used in the reproductive process and infectious copies

The hepatitis virus uses the chemical protease (model shown) to replicate itself. Scientists are trying to develop a protease inhibitor to block the virus's reproduction.

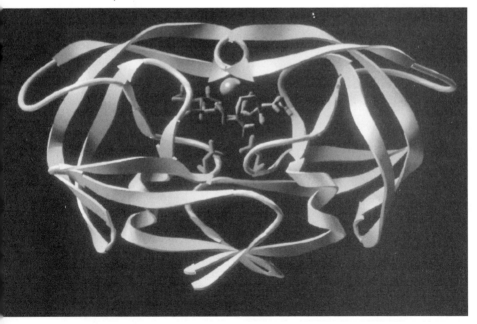

to be formed. Pharmaceutical companies have invested over $5 million to study protease inhibitors for hepatitis. These still are being evaluated in research laboratories and have not yet been tested on humans. However because protease inhibitors currently are being used successfully to treat the AIDS virus, scientists hypothesize that they will be equally effective in treating hepatitis. According to Dr. Gregory Everson, "It is likely that inhibitors will have a major impact on the treatment of hepatitis C."[64]

Learning About the Liver

While many studies are concentrating on learning about the hepatitis virus, other studies are examining the liver itself in order to develop new treatments to preserve the liver, help it to regenerate, and change liver transplant methods. In an effort to reduce the rate of death from liver disease, these studies are centering on the interaction between the hepatitis virus and liver cells, how the cells become injured, and how the liver regenerates. Some experts hypothesize that the hepatitis virus alone is not powerful enough to destroy liver cells. As a result, they are examining all the factors involved in liver cell injury and in liver repair. One study in the Kanazawa University Medical School in Japan examined liver cell injury in mice. In this study mice were injected with a chemical that caused liver injury. After being injected with the liver-damaging chemical, all the mice's ALT levels rose. One group was also injected with cytokine interleukin, a protein that is produced by the immune system to fight injury and disease. This group's ALT levels quickly normalized. A second group was injected with a chemical that prevented their bodies from producing cytokine interleukin naturally. Their ALT levels rapidly increased. Based on this study, researchers theorize that liver cell injury caused by hepatitis may be worse in people with low levels of cytokine interleukin and, conversely, may be less damaging in people with higher levels of the protein. Further studies examining interleukin's effect on liver cell injury and regeneration, and how it can be used to treat hepatitis, are ongoing. According to Dr. Gregory Everson, "In the absence of effective therapy to eradicate hepatitis, therapy that can modify basic mechanisms of cell injury may reduce the rate of progression to cirrhosis and the need for liver transplantation, slow the progression of liver failure and reduce the rate of death from liver disease."[65]

In an effort to achieve this goal, a number of studies are examining transplanting liver cells rather than whole livers to people with failing livers. In this process transplanted liver cells are used to keep patients waiting for liver transplants alive. Scientists working with this process think that transplanted healthy liver cells can do many of the jobs that diseased liver cells are no longer able to do, thus preventing or delaying liver failure.

Liver cells used in this process are currently gathered from live donors and donated livers, and are expected to be gathered from cloned animals in the future. Cells recovered from live donors are taken from living people who donate a section of their livers. These are livers that, due to injury or illness, are not acceptable for use in liver transplant but do contain some healthy cells that can be recovered. Because the liver can regenerate, the remaining part of the donor's liver and the donated part will reach the size of a normal liver within three months. The donor does not have to be related to the recipient, but must have the same blood type. It is estimated that cells from one single liver could serve twenty people. The regeneration process protects the donor from liver failure and provides a large number of liver cells for transplant.

Transplanting cloned animals cells into humans is not yet possible, but researchers predict it will be feasible in the future. This process involves cloning animals that have been genetically changed in order that their cells will not be rejected by the human immune system. Although this process is still in its early stages, genetically altered pigs have already been cloned, and scientists are quite hopeful about the use of cloned animal liver cells in the future.

Currently five centers in the United States, known as liver cell banks, are experimenting with live liver cell and donated liver cell transplants. Using a process known as cryobiology, liver cells are isolated, sterilized, and then frozen and stored in a special medium. The cells are later thawed and used in transplants.

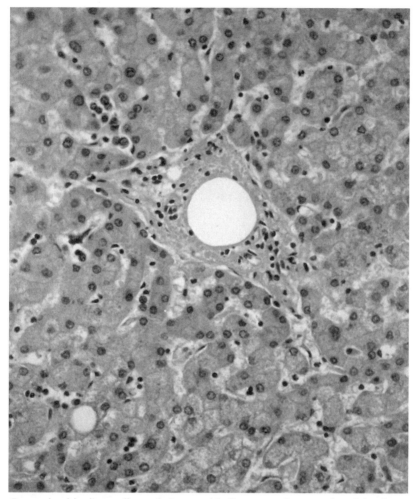

Frozen healthy liver cells are being used in liver transplants and to delay liver failure in hepatitis patients.

At the present time this process is being used to delay liver failure in hepatitis patients waiting for a new liver. However, experts are optimistic about expanding its use in the future. They theorize that since healthy liver cells can regenerate, newly transplanted liver cells should eventually spread throughout the damaged liver, making liver transplants unnecessary. Experts are optimistic that liver cell transplants could save the lives of thousands of people each year. According to Dr. Jaime Tisnado of the Medical College of Virginia, a center where liver cell transplants are being performed experimentally, "A single liver used as a source for transplantable cells could provide enough cells for twenty people or maybe more. That is significant considering the mathematics of liver transplantation: about 5000 patients receive liver transplants each year, but 15,000 are waiting for donor organs. Many of those who are waiting will die while waiting."[66]

So far, twelve patients at the Medical College of Virginia have undergone liver cell transplants. Of these eight still are alive and doing well. At another center, five patients received liver cell transplants and two survived. In one case, an eleven-year-old girl received a liver cell transplant. Unlike in liver transplant, which is long and complex, this girl was able to enter the hospital, have the liver cell transplant, and go home, all

Stem cells (below) may one day be harvested from the hepatitis patient's own bone marrow and transplanted into the liver to keep it functioning.

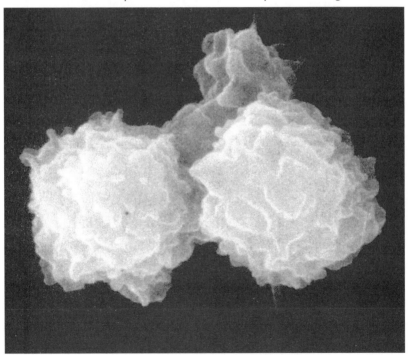

in one day. Two years later she is alive and her liver is functioning well.

Other studies are using bone marrow stem cells to replace liver cells. Stem cells are special cells found in tissues throughout the body that, scientists believe, are capable of changing into, and repairing, almost any cell in the human body. Animal studies have shown that when the liver is injured or damaged by disease, stem cells found in bone marrow routinely are changed into new liver cells and sent to the liver where they help it to regenerate. In an effort to see whether this also occurs in humans, researchers studied two women who received male bone marrow stem cell transplants stained with a special dye, which made it easy for researchers to distinguish these cells from the women's own bone marrow cells. The researchers found that the male bone marrow cells rapidly traveled to the women's livers where they formed more male liver cells. The scientists were impressed with how fast stem cells seem to multiply and rebuild the liver. According to liver regeneration expert Dr. Neville Fausto, "What is quite exciting is that the level of replacement or proliferation of bone marrow cells is quite significant. Production of liver cells of up to 40%—that is really significant."[67]

Because bone marrow stem cells are relatively easy to gather and can be kept alive outside the body, researchers predict that someday transplanted bone marrow stem cells may be used to keep a patient's liver functioning until it repairs itself. It also may be possible to harvest a person's own bone marrow stem cells and use them to build an artificial liver that can be transplanted into the person. Experts agree that if these studies are correct and transplanted stem cells can rapidly regenerate the liver, they may provide a life saving alternative for hepatitis patients in need of a liver transplant.

Other studies are attempting to combine what has been learned about liver cells with what is known about the liver to create an artificial liver that would work similarly to a kidney dialysis machine, which helps damaged kidneys remove waste products from the body. Because no similar machine currently exists to help people suffering from liver failure, scientists are seeking to develop one. Such a machine would not be implanted directly into a patient's body, instead, the patient would be hooked up to it. The patient's blood would pass through the machine, which would remove toxins from blood and add healthy liver cells to the blood. Scientists theorize that by detoxifying the blood and supplying the liver with healthy liver cells, this machine would improve liver functions and give the liver a chance to regenerate. They predict that the addition of enough healthy liver cells would cause the liver to function normally, making both a liver transplant and further use of the artificial liver unnecessary. Unfortunately, the development of a machine that could both detoxify the blood and add functioning liver cells to the body is extremely complex. Consequently, work on such a machine is highly experimental. Although the concept is promising, experts do not expect an artificial liver to be created soon.

With current research developing new and effective treatments and the prospect of the eventual development of a vaccine for hepatitis C, people with hepatitis who currently face limited and often ineffective treatments look hopefully to the future. As one patient explains:

> Although I anchor myself in the present and enjoy life day by day, I spend a lot of time worrying about the future. Will researchers perfect a protease inhibitor soon enough to help me? Will they come up with a technique that can keep a person with liver disease alive, like dialysis for patients with kidney failure? At my support group, we announce each tiny advance and permit ourselves the necessary hope. The future looks promising. All of us feel there's got to be something better coming down the pike. And we wait and hope.[68]

Notes

Introduction: A Silent Threat to Individuals and Society

1. Quoted in American Liver Foundation, "Making Every Day Count." www.liverfoundation.org.
2. Quoted in American Liver Foundation, "Making Every Day Count."

Chapter 1: What Is Hepatitis?

3. Quoted in Gregory T. Everson, M.D., and Hedy Weinberg, *Living with Hepatitis C*. New York: Hatherleigh Press, 1999, p. 8.
4. Quoted in *Health with the Web M.D.*, "Hepatitis C." www.content.health.msn.com.
5. Steve, interview with the author, Dallas, Texas, November 8, 2001.
6. Leland, interview with the author, Dallas, Texas, January 3, 2002.
7. Quoted in *Sandi's Crusade Against Hepatitis C*, "Deb's Story." http://members.rogers.com.
8. Rose, interview with the author, Dallas, Texas, December 1, 2001.
9. Quoted in *Canadian Press*, "Hepatitis C More Prevalent and Easier to Contract than HIV," October 2, 2001.
10. Quoted in Everson and Weinberg, *Living with Hepatitis C*, p. 38.
11. Quoted in *Sandi's Crusade Against Hepatitis*, "Irene's Story." http://members.rogers.com.

12. Quoted in *Hepatitis Weekly*, "Virginia Sixth Grader Will Need Hepatitis Shots To Enroll in School," July 2, 2001, p. 10.

13. Quoted in Everson and Weinberg, *Living with Hepatitis C*, p. 41.

14. Quoted in Everson and Weinberg, *Living with Hepatitis C*, p. 41.

Chapter 2: Diagnosis and Treatment

15. Melissa Palmer, *Dr. Melissa Palmer's Guide to Hepatitis and Liver Disease*. Garden City Park, NY: Avery Publishing, 2000, p. 107.

16. Marie, interview with the author, Dallas, Texas, December 13, 2001.

17. Quoted in Matthew Dolan, *Hepatitis C Handbook*. Berkeley, CA: North Atlantic Books, 1999, p. 39.

18. Steve, interview with the author.

19. Quoted in *Sandi's Crusade Against Hepatitis C*, "Lisa's Story." http://members.rogers.com.

20. Quoted in Everson and Weinberg, *Living with Hepatitis C*, p. 137.

21. Palmer, *Dr. Melissa Palmer's Guide*, p. 167.

22. Quoted in *Sandi's Crusade Against Hepatitis C*, "Peter's Story." http://members.rogers.com.

23. Quoted in Everson and Weinberg, *Living with Hepatitis C*, p. 142.

24. Quoted in Prithi Yelaja, "The Waiting List Is So Long. If I Don't Get a New Liver, I Die," *Toronto Star*, September 20, 2001, p. 25.

25. Quoted in *Hepatitis C Forum*, "Uncle Dave: My Hepatitis Story." www.hepatitis-c.de/uncldave.htm.

26. Quoted in Everson and Weinberg, *Living with Hepatitis C*, p. 161.

27. Quoted in *Ask Emilyss Monthly Online Magazine*, "A Conversation with David Crosby—His HCV Story, His Liver Trans-

plant and Now," December 2001. www.askemilyss.com.

28. Quoted in *Hepatitis C Forum*, "Uncle Dave: My Hepatitis Story."

Chapter 3: Alternative Treatments

29. Marie, interview with the author.

30. Quoted in Dolan, *Hepatitis C Handbook*, p. 109.

31. Keivan Jinnah, "Natural Therapies for Hepatitis C with Keivan Jinnah, N.D., M.S.O.M., L.A.C.," WebMD Health. http://my.webmd.com.

32. Marie, interview with the author.

33. Carson Burgstiner, "This Is Why I Started Taking These Vitamins." www.acts238.net.

34. Quoted in *A Doctor in your House*, "Other Health Issues Hepatitis C." www.adoctorinyourhouse.com.

35. Alan Berkman, *Hepatitis A to G.* New York: Warner Books, 2000, p. 145.

36. Quoted in Everson and Weinberg, *Living with Hepatitis C*, p. 82.

37. Marie, interview with the author.

Chapter 4: Living with Hepatitis

38. Quoted in Dolan, *Hepatitis C Handbook*, p. 171.

39. Quoted in Everson and Weinberg, *Living with Hepatitis C*, p. 67.

40. Everson and Weinberg, *Living with Hepatitis C*, p. 88.

41. Quoted in Everson and Weinberg, *Living with Hepatitis C*, p. 69.

42. *Sandi's Crusade Against Hepatitis C*, "HCV–The Taboo Subject." http://members.rogers.com.

43. Quoted in Everson and Weinberg, *Living with Hepatitis C*, p. 8.

44. Mandy Appleyard, "Live for Today," *Daily Record*, Glasgow,

Scotland, October 10, 2001, p. 4.

45. Quoted in *Sandi's Crusade Against Hepatitis C*, "Peter's Story."

46. Quoted in Dolan, *Hepatitis C Handbook*, p. 161.

47. Palmer, *Dr. Melissa Palmer's Guide*, p. 335.

48. Quoted in Everson and Weinberg, *Living with Hepatitis C*, p. 87.

49. Leland, interview with the author.

50. Quoted in Everson and Weinberg, *Living with Hepatitis C*, p. 89.

51. Appleyard, "Live for Today," p. 4.

52. Palmer, *Dr. Melissa Palmer's Guide*, p. 382.

53. Quoted in *Ask Emilyss Monthly Online Magazine*, "Living With HCV," July 2001. www.askemilyss.com.

54. Quoted in Dolan, *Hepatitis C Handbook*, p. 138.

55. Palmer, *Dr. Melissa Palmer's Guide*, p. 361.

56. Quoted in *A Doctor in Your House*, "Other Health Issues Hepatitis C."

57. Leland, interview with the author.

Chapter 5: What the Future Holds

58. Kenneth B. Chiacchia, "Looking To The Future," *HepNet*. www.hepnet.com.

59. Everson, and Weinberg, *Living with Hepatitis C*, p. 218.

60. Quoted in *Hepatitis Central*, "Rx for B and C." www.hepatitis-central.com.

61. Quoted in *HepC Research*, "Pegasys Plus Ribavirin Significantly More Effective than International Standard of Care for Treatment of Hepatitis C." www.hepcresearch.com.

62. Quoted in Daniel DeNoon, "New Hepatitis C Combo Treatment Is a 'Cure' for Many," *Health with WebMD*. http://content.health.msn.com.

63. Quoted in *Hepatitis Central*, "Rx for B and C."

64. Everson and Weinberg, *Living with Hepatitis C*, p. 218.

65. Everson and Weinberg, *Living with Hepatitis C*, p. 220.

66. Quoted in Neil Osterweil, "Experimental Treatments May Delay Liver Failure," *Health with WebMD*. http://content.health.msn.com.

67. Quoted in Daniel DeNoon, "Bone Marrow Helps Rebuild Liver, Opens Door to New Treatments," *Health with WebMD*. http://content.health.msn.com.

68. Quoted in Everson and Weinberg, *Living with Hepatitis C*, p. 211.

Glossary

acute disease: A disease that lasts six months or less and then disappears.

ALT: A chemical called alanine aminotransferase that is produced when the liver is inflamed.

anesthesiologist: A doctor who gives the patient anesthetics during surgery.

anesthetic: A drug that causes numbness.

antibody: A protein produced by the body to fight bacteria and viruses.

antioxidant: Substance that helps the body fight disease and eliminate poisons.

asymptomatic carriers: People who are infected with an infectious disease but have no symptoms.

bile: A chemical produced by the liver that helps to neutralize poisons and digest fats.

bilirubin: A yellow chemical produced by the liver.

biopsy: The removal of a small piece of tissue that is examined for the presence of disease.

blood-borne disease: A disease spread through contact with infected blood.

chronic disease: An incurable disease that may last throughout a person's life.

cirrhosis: A disease that causes scarring of the liver.

cryobiology: The study of the freezing of living cells to be used for scientific purposes.

dialysis: A medical procedure used to treat people with kidney disease.

diuretic: A medication that helps the body eliminate excess fluids.

DNA: Deoxyribonucleic acid, a part of genes that carries hereditary information.

encephalopathy: A condition of the liver caused by excess protein; it causes mental confusion and drowsiness.

enzyme: A protein produced by the body; it produces chemical changes.

glutathione: A chemical that protects the liver from damage from toxins.

glycogen: A chemical that the liver makes from carbohydrates and releases into the blood in order to provide the body with energy.

hepatitis: An inflammation or infection of the liver caused by a virus.

hepatologist: A doctor who specializes in the liver.

herbs: Plants with healing properties.

immunosuppressant: A drug that keeps the immune system from attacking transplanted organs.

infectious: contagious.

integrative treatment: Combining conventional and alternative treatments.

liver failure: When the liver is no longer able to function.

milk thistle: An herb used to treat hepatitis.

mutation: A permanent change in a gene.

nicotine: A chemical found in cigarettes.

regenerate: Grow back.

reproduce: Multiply or form copies of oneself.

RNA: Ribonucleic acid, a part of genes that carries hereditary information.

silymarin: A chemical found in the herb milk thistle that is believed to strengthen the liver.

toxins: Poisons.

unprotected sex: Having sex without using a condom, which protects against the exchange of body fluids.

viral load: The amount of hepatitis virus found in the blood.

Organizations to Contact

American Liver Foundation
1425 Pompton Ave.
Cedar Grove, NJ 07009-1000
(800) 465-4837
e-mail: webmail@liverfoundation.org
www.liverfoundation.org

This nonprofit organization provides educational material, support, and information for people with all types of liver disease. It also funds research studies on liver disease and gives information about clinical trials.

Hepatitis Foundation International
30 Sunrise Terrace
Cedar Grove, NJ 07009-1423
(800) 891-0707
e-mail: HFI@intac.com
www.hepfi.org

This international organization provides information on every aspect of hepatitis. It offers online support, chat groups, and advice for coping.

National Hepatitis C Coalition
P.O. Box 1302
Fallbrook, CA 92028
(760) 451-3437
www.nationalhepatitis-c.org

This nonprofit organization, a national coalition of hepatitis C patients and their families, offers education and support and online communication, notice of hepatitis-related events, member stories, and links.

National Institute of Allergy and Infectious Diseases
NIAID Office of Communications
Building 31
Room 7A50
Bethesda, MD 20892
(301) 496-5717
www.niaid.nih.gov

This organization sponsors research studies on hepatitis. It provides informational packets, fact sheets, press releases, and information about research.

Transplant Recipient International Organization
1000 16th St. NW
Suite 602
Washington, DC 20036-5705
(800) TRIO-386
www.trioweb.org

This international organization provides information and support for transplant patients and their loved ones.

For Further Reading

Books

Virginia Aronson, *Everything You Need to Know About Hepatitis.* New York: Rosen Publishing, 2000. Explains what hepatitis is, how to avoid contracting it, and its effect on people.

Ann Beyers, *Sexually Transmitted Diseases.* Berkeley Heights, NJ: Enslow Publishers, 1999. Discusses a number of sexually transmitted diseases including hepatitis.

Misha Ruth Cohen, *The Hepatitis C Help Book.* New York: St. Martin's Press, 2000. Provides information on different alternative treatments including using nutrition, exercise, and Asian treatments to help fight hepatitis C.

Gregory T. Everson, *Living with Hepatitis B.* New York: Hatherleigh Press, 2000. Discusses every aspect of hepatitis B with numerous statements from patients. It provides strategies to help sufferers cope.

Virginia Alvin Silverstein and Robert Silverstein, *Hepatitis.* Berkely Heights, NJ: Enslow Publishers 1994. Covers how hepatitis is spread, the history of the disease, and the symptoms and treatments.

Harriet Washington, *Living Healthy with Hepatitis C.* New York: Dell, 2000. Offers many strategies to help hepatitis C sufferers cope.

Websites

Ask Emilyss (www.askemilyss.com).

Ask Noah About Hepatitis (www.noah-health.org).

Hepatitis Neighborhood (www.hepatitisneighborhood.com.

HepC Research (www.hepcresearch.com).

HepNet (www.hepnet.com).

Sandi's Crusade Against Hepatitis C (http://members.rogers. com).

Works Consulted

Books

Alan Berkman, *Hepatitis A to G*. New York: Warner Books, 2000. Provides details on all seven types of hepatitis.

Matthew Dolan, *Hepatitis C Handbook*. Berkeley, CA: North Atlantic Books, 1999. Very informative book on every aspect of hepatitis C. It provides details on many forms of alternative treatment.

Gregory T. Everson, M.D., and Hedy Weinberg, *Living with Hepatitis C*. New York: Hatherleigh Press, 1999. Gives good information on what hepatitis C is, how it is transmitted, diagnosed and treated, and gives tips to help people with hepatitis C cope. It also contains many statements from patients.

Melissa Palmer, *Dr. Melissa Palmer's Guide to Hepatitis and Liver Disease*. Garden City Park, NY: Avery Publishing, 2000. Focuses on the liver and how it functions. It talks about the different types of hepatitis as well as other diseases of the liver. It discusses liver transplant procedures in detail.

Periodicals

Mandy Appleyard, "Live for Today," *Daily Record*, Glasgow, Scotland, October 10, 2001.

Canadian Press, "Hepatitis C More Prevalent and Easier to Contract than HIV," October 2, 2001.

Hepatitis Weekly, "Virginia Sixth Grader Will Need Hepatitis Shots To Enroll In School," July 2, 2001.

Prithi Yelaja, "The Waiting List Is So Long. If I Don't Get a New Liver, I Die," *Toronto Star*, September 20, 2001.

Internet Sources

American Liver Foundation, "Making Every Day Count." www.liverfoundation.org.

Ask Emilyss Monthly Online Magazine, "A Conversation with David Crosby—His HCV Story, His Liver Transplant and Now," December 2001. www.askemilyss.com.

Ask Emilyss Monthly Online Magazine, "Living With HCV," July 2001. www.askemilyss.com.

Carson Burgstiner, "This Is Why I Started Taking These Vitamins." www.acts238.net.

Kenneth B. Chiacchia, "Looking To The Future," *HepNet.* www.hepnet.com.

Daniel DeNoon, "Bone Marrow Helps Rebuild Liver, Opens Door to New Treatments," *Health with WebMD.* http://content.health.msn.com.

————, "New Hepatitis C Combo Treatment Is a 'Cure' for Many," *Health with WebMD.* http://content.health.msn.com.

A Doctor in Your House, "Other Health Issues Hepatitis C." www.adoctorinyourhouse.com.

Health with the Web M.D., "Hepatitis C." www.content.health.msn.com.

Hepatitis C Forum, "Uncle Dave: My Hepatitis Story." www.hepatitis-c.de/uncldave.htm.

Hepatitis Central, "Rx for B and C." www.hepatitis-central.com.

HepC Research, "Pegasys Plus Ribavirin Significantly More Effective than International Standard of Care for Treatment of Hepatitis C." www.hepcresearch.com.

Keivan Jinnah, "Natural Therapies for Hepatitis C with Keivan Jinnah, N.D., M.S.O.M., L.A.C.," *WebMD Health.* http://my.webmd.com.

Neil Osterweil, "Experimental Treatments May Delay Liver Failure," *Health with WebMD.* http://content.health.msn.com.

Sandi's Crusade Against Hepatitis C, "Deb's Story," http://members. rogers.com.

————, "HCV-The Taboo Subject," http://members.rogers.com.

————, "Irene's Story." http://members.rogers.com.

————, "Lisa's Story." http://members.rogers.com.

————, "Peter's Story." http://members.rogers.com.

Index

Picture Credits

About the Author

Barbara Sheen has been a writer and educator for more than thirty years. Her writing has been published in the United States and Europe. She writes in both English and Spanish, and has a masters of science degree. She currently lives in Texas with her family, where she enjoys weight lifting, reading, and cooking. This is her third book in the Diseases and Disorders series.